MW00826471

Charles Bass

Life on the Shiny Iron

Memories of a Mid-Century Brakeman

Charles Bass

Life on the Shiny Iron

Memories of a Mid-Century Brakeman

Falconart Media LLC
Middleton, Wisconsin U.S.A.

All photographs are by the author unless otherwise credited

Text and photo layout and cover design by George Allez
on a Mac mini computer using QuarkXPress v. 7.0.1

Thanks to Tom Jacobson, Chicago & North Western engineer,
for sharing his knowledge of steam and diesel engines

Front cover photograph courtesy of William F. Armstrong

Printing and binding by **Park Printing Ltd.** *Verona, Wisconsin U.S.A.*

The text is set in Century Schoolbook, designed by Morris Fuller Benton in 1919
for American Type Founders

Library of Congress Control Number: 2008942013

ISBN-13: 978-0-9740804-6-8
ISBN-10: 0-9740804-6-2

10   9   8   7   6   5   4   3   2   1

ALL RIGHTS RESERVED

Copyright © Charles Bass
M M I X

to

My grandfather, **Ben Bass,** *conductor*

My father, **Roger Bass,** *conductor*

My brother, **John Bass**

 thanks for the memories

1

IN 1950 I graduated from West High in Madison, Wisconsin. Unlike most of my classmates I didn't have the money to go to college and, like most graduates, not much in the way of job skills. A week or two after graduation, Dad, who was a brakeman and conductor on the Chicago & North Western, asked me if I'd like to go to work as a relief clerk at the North Western depot. Apparently he had a lot of pull with the station master, Mr. Jorgenson. So I looked over my hand and considered all my option — that's not a typo — and took the job, the start of a promising career.

The depot was a very large building and is now the home of Madison Gas & Electric. It was built in an era when there were separate waiting rooms for the ladies, to protect their delicate sensibilities from the crude, boisterous, cigar smoking, tobacco chewing men in the main waiting room. It even had spittoons. There was a lunchroom that was usual for large depots. In an area between the lunchroom and the waiting room was the Union News stand with all the magical smells of worldly pulp fiction novels with romantic covers, detective stories, magazines, newspapers, post cards, and souvenirs. I swept and mopped the depot and freight house floors the old-fashioned way, with a mop and a bucket

New Madison Depot early 1900's.

of water. I also swept the platforms, picked up trash and did all the usual things a custodian, er, facilities manager does. Along with the job I had to become a member of the Brotherhood of Railroad Clerks.

During the course of my duties I saw a mix of head end power ranging from very old steam engines to the then modern diesels. The oldest engine type I saw was the Class D Atlantic which pulled train 620 from Madison

Don Ross collection

Class D Atlantic high wheeler. It has an expanded coal bunker.

Don Ross collection

Class E-4 Hudson

to Milwaukee daily and train 601 on the return trip. My grandfather made his last run on that job. Many D's were used in commuter service out of Chicago.

These engines were built from 1900 to 1907 and served until the early 1950's. They had a 4-4-2 wheel arrangement, four pilot wheels or pony trucks, four drivers and two trailing wheels. They were not a real robust engine but very fast. They had huge drive wheels, 83 inches, which is three inches higher than the doors in your home. And that isn't counting the flanges. Appropriately they were called high wheelers.

The only North Western steam engines that had taller drivers were the nine Hudson E-4's that were built in 1938. These engines were streamlined or shrouded and looked very sleek and modern. They gave the trains an upscale look but I think I would have preferred to see the black iron. The Hudson type engines, unshrouded, were handsome and with their 4-6-4 wheel arrangement were very well proportioned.

Some Pacifics were also shrouded but their design didn't turn out nearly as good as the Hudson's. The E-4 Hudsons were too heavy for the Madison line. Their drivers were three inches taller than the high wheeler D's. I would liked to have seen what those engines looked like without their streamlined sheet metal but no picture of them exists that I know of. The North Western's were the heaviest of that type in the nation.

I was starting my railroad career on the bottom rung, going from the ground up, a strong base for great success in the years to come. My fervent hope at the time was that this was the career track that all the great Railroad Robber Barons followed.

The freight house must have been built around the turn of the century, a solid red brick building. The office area was too full of old desks and chairs, shelves, baskets full of papers and waste baskets. And calendars and cigar and cigarette ashes. The freight house had inside rail docks. Steel plates spanned the space between the floor and the cars. There were

Madison depot in 1950 after I swept the platform. The freight house is the building on the far left.

no fork lifts or pallet jacks. Everything was handled by large, heavy hand trucks or heavier dollies. The regular guys had paid their dues in the freight house or somewhere else on the railroad and were all on the back side of the curve. If I'd stuck with the railroad, who knows?

One of the most important functions of the freight house was handling less than carload or LCL shipments. Large shippers ordered the cars they needed for their goods and the cars would be spotted and loaded at their facilities. Examples of these products would be lumber, grain, coal, oil, and so on. Smaller shipments were combined with other shippers' products at the freight house to load the LCL cars. All depots served the LCL function on a much smaller scale for the local businesses. Most depots had what was called a house track behind the depot leading to a platform that was used for loading and unloading heavy items and machinery. In earlier times it was also known as the team track. LCL cars were spotted on the house track to be loaded or unloaded while the train crew was switching the town.

In the mid-50's the railroads were handling a lot of U.S. mail and one of my jobs was to help sort outgoing parcel post that came down from the post office. About eight wagons were positioned back to back and side by side. The post office truck backed up to them and the driver handed us the mail sacks. Each town had a specific location on the wagons, usually one town in front and one in back. I didn't work that job steady enough to learn the towns or their spots on the wagons and I felt pretty stupid asking where the same town goes three times in about three minutes. To make it worse

Madison depot interior that I mopped occasionally and swept often. The door behind the man is the entrance to Union News and the restaurant. The window to the left is the ticket office.
Wisconsin State Historical Society #33391

the town with the depot often served surrounding towns so you needed to remember the names of more than one town for each spot.

I loaded and unloaded passenger luggage on the trains, redcapped when I was on janitorial duty, sorted internal company mail and did other similarly important duties. The luggage cart that I used for redcapping has been restored and is currently on display at the Mid-Continental Museum in North Freedom (I asked to have it bronzed). Since I was a relief man, at various times I worked all three shifts.

Luggage cart

After we'd sorted the mail for train 511, which was coming out of Chicago, we pulled the wagons over to the platform beside the track, lined them up and waited. The mail handlers were mostly guys that were not real ambitious or were waiting for something better to come along. One man had his name in to be a City of Madison fireman, a job which he eventually got. These men came and went. That job was not a career opportunity.

We had a pretty good idea when 511, a heavy passenger train, was going to arrive because the ticket office clerk got the word from the dispatcher, the god of train control, upstairs in the depot. On some nights the dispatcher was Augie Troia. Five eleven was almost always on time. Looking east we finally saw the gyrating beam from the engine's Mars light slashing the night sky doing figure 8's, getting higher and brighter in the sky. The Mars light was invented by the guy who invented that candy bar. The train would be rolling over the trestle across Monona Bay, clattering over the diamond where the C & NW crossed the Milwaukee Road tracks in the middle of the bay and then the lights would disappear.

Some minutes later and a few hundred yards down the track the lights suddenly reappear with great intensity, the head light staring blindingly, the Mars light oscillating wildly.

Don Ross collection

Westbound freight passing MX Tower approaching the diamond in Monona Bay. Train 511 would follow that evening.

The engines stopped at the Blair Street crossing. The door of the crossing guard's little shed at the edge of Blair Street popped open and he came out with a stop sign held high, swinging his red lantern. He was short and fat and looked like one of Snow White's dwarfs, I'm thinking Grumpy. It was his moment of triumph! The engine bell started to ring. He proceeded to walk across the street stopping traffic, and the huge engines, bell clanging, obediently followed. After the last car cleared the street the little man disappeared into his little shed and closed the door. It was a cuckoo clock scenario.

One day a steam engine pulled up to the Blair Street crossing and the crossing guard did not come out. So the engineer pulled into the street and was promptly hit by a car. Asked about it, the engineer said if the guy couldn't see his engine he probably wouldn't have seen the crossing guard.

Train 511, the Duluth-Superior Limited, was probably the most popular North Western passenger train that came into Madison. It left Chicago early in the evening, bringing home local people who had transferred from trains that came into Chicago depots from places all over the country or who had spent a day or two in Chicago shopping or on business. There was a regular service called Parmalee Transfer that moved passengers and luggage between depots in Chicago, primarily between the huge Union Station and the North Western depot. The name had a nice ring to it. Five eleven arrived at a decent hour, 9:38 p.m. We had twelve minutes to unload and load baggage and mail.

The train had an RPO car (Railway Post Office). The guys in the RPO cars always carried guns. Remember Sam Bass, notorious outlaw who stole $60,000 from a Union Pacific train? Sam's interest in trains was commendable but a little over the top. He stole more money from the Union Pacific than any other train robber. That's not counting the Railroad Robber Barons. He died of lead poisoning. He was not a relative. At least we don't think so. And then there were the James boys.

In the late 1950's mail started to gravitate from trains to contracted truckers, star routes. That was a big loss to the railroads because carrying the mail was very profitable for them. By the early 60's railroads were pretty much out of the mail and passenger business.

The last car on the train was used exclusively for passengers traveling from Chicago to Madison and stations in between but not beyond. All passengers in this car got off at Madison and the car would be cut off and left. Many of the passengers were quite well dressed and they were the best redcap tippers, sometimes twenty-five cents a bag. Where else could you make that kind of money?

The rear brakeman disconnected his signal hose and took down the two red and green marker lights from the back of the Madison car and carried them up to the rear of the next car and attached them. Meanwhile the car men, commonly referred to as car knockers, were disconnecting the steam and air lines ahead of the Madison car. When the train was ready to depart, the brakeman or the car knocker pulled the pin on what was now the last coach, leaving the Madison coach sitting on the main as the train went out of town. The switch crew moved the car to a side track. It would be cleaned and put on an eastbound train to Chicago the next day.

Working 511 on Thursday nights was a hard job. That's the night Life Magazines came to town. They were bagged in tall narrow parcel post sacks and were basically just a two and a half foot stack of magazines. The bags had draw strings on top and were called slugs. At the time, I weighed about one hundred forty five pounds, so weight-wise a slug and I were about an even match, or at least it seemed that way. There were supposed to be weight limits on these bags but nobody was real strict about following them. The baggageman in the car grabbed each bag by the strings and dragged it over to the door. The mail wagon was positioned beside the car and was a couple feet lower than the baggage car floor. This was now decision time for him: does he stand the bag up for me or just hand me the strings to drag the bag out of the car and stand it up? Most of the time I got the strings. In fairness, most of these guys were older and maybe some weren't up to picking them up. How come I always got the car with the slugs? After spending some time picking up those bags and stacking them on the wagon I was very happy to see 511's marker lights silently pass by on its way out of town. Next stop for them, Lodi. Our next job was loading the slugs on post office trucks going uptown. And finally seeing the truck tail lights not so silently disappear in the dark. The truck was an old World War II open rack 4 x 4.

Train 515, the Victory, was a heavy mail train. It arrived in Madison at 11:46 p.m. and departed at 12:10 a.m. so we had to have the mail sorted and wagons spotted on the platform before it came in. Sometimes we had to jockey slow moving baggage wagons beside the faster moving rail cars at the same time. We had to get them out of town in twenty-four minutes. We used a small yellow tug that always almost wouldn't start but did to haul the wagons to the platform. We pulled five or six at a time, weaving through the I-beams that held up the platform roof. You had to plan your course very carefully or the last wagon wouldn't clear one of them. When you hit one it rang pretty good. Part of your status was your skill avoiding columns when you were driving the tug pulling a string of wagons to the baggage cars. Those little things added up.

While we were loading and unloading the baggage cars the train's engines were cut off from the train and moved forward past the cross-over switches. The switch engine standing by came through the cross-overs, grabbed two or three heavyweight baggage cars off the front of the train and spotted them over on the track next to the alley behind the depot. Then the train's engines backed onto their train again and whenever we were done, hopefully by 12:10, the marker lights again silently passed by. After 515 left we went over to the baggage cars that had been set out, lit the gas lights and went to work. These bags were very large but not as heavy as slugs. Same truck driver, back and forth to the post office. It took awhile to get those cars unloaded.

At Christmas time we had additional work loading out bags of Swiss Colony Cheese. They shipped a huge amount of their product during the holiday season and cheese is very heavy. The parcel post sacks were very large. Swiss Colony is still located in Monroe, Wisconsin.

Skid row in Madison was on Blair Street across from the depot. The term "skid row" came from the timber industry in the Pacific Northwest. The downed trees in the forests had to be dragged by horses or oxen to a river so they could be floated downstream to the saw mills. Dragging trunks over the uneven ground was very difficult at best so the lumberjacks laid logs cross-wise on the muddy paths and dragged the freshly cut timber down their new skid row. Where the skid row met the water, enterprising people determined that there could be a need for various types of highly profitable enterprises, some of which could really make a feller's day. But that's another story.

The term came into general use to describe the gathering place for the most serious down-and-outers in an area. Madison Street in Chicago, from the depot going west, was a prime example. At times some of the men in those places served an important function for the railroads. In extremely heavy snow storms the railroads would send buses down there looking for men to help shovel out switches to keep the trains running. One of the requirements for those jobs was that they had to have shoes. The pay was not great. After a huge snow storm in the late 40's a bunch of those guys were brought to Milwaukee to help clear the snow but many couldn't handle it and went back to Chicago. We know today that many of them were traumatized war veterans and there was no infrastructure to help them. Not everyone could come back from war and go on with his life. These veterans would have been World War II men.

The center-piece of Madison's skid row was the infamous "400 Bar," the sleaziest bar in town, patronized by hard core professional down-and-outers. It was directly across Blair Street from the depot's main entrance. Late at night patrons came out of the bar looking for a place to sleep or get out of the cold. If they could get there, that place was usually the depot where they would stretch out on the benches or on the marble floor. Part of my job was suggesting to them that they find lodging elsewhere. They were usually pretty compliant. On cold nights I wouldn't do that. The hardest part was dealing with some of the stuff they left behind in the restrooms. That was sometimes a nasty job and you don't want to know the details. One of the important things I learned from that task was that there was no job I was too good to do.

One of my chores was to walk down a string of cars in Monona Yard and do I'm not sure what. On one end of each car was a totally indecipherable code scribbled in chalk. The clerk I was with read it and wrote something down on a list he was carrying. He was tall, soft-spoken and apparently not very judgmental, and had been up and down the yard a few times and looked it. The markings were used to make up a switch list, giving the location of each car and where it was to be switched or spotted. I think at times he may have made scribbles of his own on the cars which were just as

unreadable. I had the feeling that I should stick to handling mail.

The other important job I had, along with the scribbler, was to check the heaters in refrigerator cars. These cars had bunkers or voids in each end which were a little less than four feet long. The cars were 36 feet long, then 40 feet, and finally they went to 50 feet. The ice bunkers on each end used up about 8 feet of the length of the car. They were heavily insulated and were used to carry perishable goods. Western railroads had a slew of these cars to carry fruit and vegetables from the west coast to all points east. Often whole trains consisted of refrigerator cars and they got expedited service.

Refrigerator cars were easily identifiable. They had two hatches over each bunker for access into the spaces below. The North Western used cars that were owned by another company, the North Western Refrigerator Line Company. Their car designation was N.W.X. followed by the car number. The X meant the cars were for use only by the car's owner or those designated by him. The North Western reefers were maintained and stored in Baraboo. That facility is now owned by the Circus World Museum and is used to house the museum's rail cars.

In January, my partner and I climbed to the top of these cars, opened the hatches and checked to make sure the kerosene heaters below were working. The compartments were heated in winter to keep the car's contents from freezing and in summer they were filled with blocks of ice to keep the products cool. They were a pain in the neck for the railroads who had to build massive storage and loading facilities to handle the ice that was needed in the summer. In winter you had to climb the ladder to the top of the car in snow and ice, edge over to the hatches and open them. The bunkers could be dangerous, filled with kerosene fumes if the heater was working. Since we never had to service a dead heater I don't know what was involved to pull out the heater and refill and

Refrigerator cars, 1920's – 50's

light it. What would OSHA think about all that? Actually, today nobody can even get on top of rail cars. The ladders don't go to the tops any more. Modern reefers have their own self-powered heating and cooling units.

The North Western rails got to Milwaukee in the early 1850's. At the time there were a number of major breweries there, Pabst, Schlitz, Blatz, and later, Miller. Apparently at that time breweries were shipping beer to Chicago on lake boats. Wagons were way too slow. The line to Chicago gave them an opportunity to move beer faster by rail. Initially they probably shipped beer in cold weather and then in the mid-1850's somebody thought of putting ice on the floor of the rail cars to keep the beer cool in warm weather. Then somebody else won the Employee of the Month Award for suggesting the bunker idea at the ends of each car.

In the mid-1800's the railroads had to build very large storage sheds to hold ice for use in the summer months and they also had to build extensive ice loading facilities to fill the bunkers in the reefers as needed. The ice was good for a couple of days and then it had to be replenished. The Great Lakes and inland lakes were a great source of water for the required quantities of ice. Mechanical refrigeration wouldn't come for another hundred years.

Cattle from the west were shipped by rail to Chicago and other meat packing centers. It was labor intensive. There were strict rules as to how long livestock could be kept in cars and how often they had to be fed and watered. The cattlemen sent their own stockmen on these trains to handle those chores. To accommodate them, railroads provided drovers' cabooses.

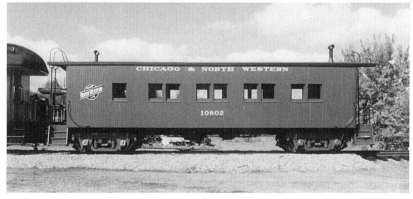

Drovers' caboose

In the North Western's case, these were basically standard wood cabooses, extended and equipped with bunks so they could handle as many men as needed to tend the cattle and still accommodate the trainmen.

Sometime later, Western cattlemen figured that rather then ship their beef on the hoof to Chicago by rail, they could slaughter their beef in the west and send the carcasses east in these newfangled refrigerator cars. However, live cattle were still shipped by rail until at least the mid-1950's. Madison crews often got a week-end stock turn down to the southwest part of the state to pick up livestock for Oscar Mayer or Cudahy Packing in Milwaukee.

One evening in late fall of 1950 I was outside the depot on the empty platform, probably sweeping up. It was dark and I noticed a headlight approaching from the west. It was train 594, a time freight eastbound for the North Western's Proviso Yard, the largest railroad yard in the country at the time. The Proviso Yard was located west of Chicago in a town called Bellwood and was subdivided into nine separate but connected yards. The receiving yard was Yard 9. There were usually six or eight orange Oscar Mayer refrigerator cars blocked on the head end of 594 right behind the engines. Folks in Proviso were waiting for those cars. They would be switched out and put on other trains outbound to other parts of the country. Train 594 and other scheduled freights were class two trains. Passenger trains were class one; apparently extras and work trains were not classified.

Anyway, the arrival of 594 at Blair Street at about 6:30 in the evening was a routine occurrence and I didn't pay much attention to it. But as it got closer I didn't hear the usual sounds of the old Class J steam engines, side rods clanking and the smoky breathing sounds of the engine's air compressor. As the train stopped at the Blair Street crossing I heard the low rumble of diesel engines idling smoothly. It was a three unit lash-up of the new General Motors Electo-Motive Division GP7 diesel-electric engines, demonstrators that would prove to the railroads that these engines could replace their steam locomotives. They were the sound of the future, the end of steam.

2

IN the summer of 1950 I did have a good two weeks, more or less, in Monona Yard, the North Western switching yard in Madison. On the other side of the main lines from the yard office was a small shed for the switch tender. There were a couple of aspects to my job. The most important one was to make sure that the switches on the west end of the yard leading to the main lines were aligned for the main so the passenger trains had a clear track when they were due. The switchmen handled the switches on the east end of the yard, sometimes not too well, as will be seen later.

There was a small indicator outside the door. It had a little arm that was normally at a forty-five degree angle. Somewhere west  of the yard and east of Waunakee there was a sensor that detected the presence of an east-bound train. When the engine hit the sensor, the indicator arm would go to horizontal, or red eye. The time card showed when the passenger trains were due so I knew when I had to pay particular attention to my little friend. The track from Waunakee to Monona Yard was downhill and fast and the inbound engineers wanted to see all semaphore signals ahead straight up and green. My other main task was to line up the switches to the yard lead for the switch engines when they came back from their downtown switching duties. I found out later that the switch crews were responsible for the switches on the east end. I missed that in my job description. Brakemen on inbound freight trains lined up the switches to yard their trains.

When I went out to the yard job there was a problem. The switch tender's job in the yard belonged to the Brotherhood of Railroad Clerks, not the switchmen's union. The switchmen felt very strongly that this job rightly belonged to them since the yards were their turf and when the regular clerk took his two week vacation they decided to make an issue about it and try to get their own guy in. Things became very tense at job grades above mine and dad was closely and angrily involved. I don't know the details but I stayed in the little house beside the tracks. So how happy were the switchmen?

In one incident the switch engine was coming back from switching downtown, cab end toward the yard and the switchmen were on the engine platform. I knew I had a critical, if not hostile, audience. I lined the main line switch to the yard lead and then went back to the next switch to open or close a switch for whichever one of the yard tracks they wanted to go into. They started waving their arms and shouting which I took as a clear indication they wanted me to do something. I couldn't hear their words, thankfully, but they were giving me a number of conflicting signals. Leave the switch open, close the switch! I took this taunting personally and decided the worst thing I could do was derail the engine.

When I started my career I remember Dad telling me that if you don't know what to do don't do anything. I still haven't worked out in my mind if that theory always works but in this case I didn't do anything. I just stepped back. The worst thing that could have happened was that they would go down the yard lead, no harm done. They'd just have to back up and we'd try it all over again. I suppose their dream was for me to throw the switch under the engine and derail it, the old *we-told-you-so* to the brass. That was the only incident. Actually once I had lined the switches for the yard lead I should have gone back to my duty station. The yard switches were their responsibility.

Other than that it was a pretty good two weeks. The weather was great and the job was not real demanding. My guess is that the job went to the clerks because it was pretty simple and, at least in my case, required no on-the-job training. And switchmen made a lot more than clerks so I think the railroad had it right.

The pictures on the next page show what could happen when the main wasn't cleared for the Dakota 400 at Monona Yard. The yard switch engine had a string of cars moving to the east end of the yard. Most cars in switch yards don't have air in their cylinders, so all braking is done by the switch engine or, as necessary, by a switchman. Because of the weight of the drag the engine couldn't stop before it fouled the main and the 400 sideswiped the switch engine. The yard track didn't have a derail, which would have saved the day. There were no injuries. The switch engineer was given some time off to spend at his favorite fishing hole.

For more than a century the railroads had been designed to handle steam power. All the necessary infrastructure was in place including the highly visible coal chutes and water towers. Railroads could easily maintain, repair, or even build new steam engines but keeping steam engines running was very labor intensive. Later a few companies built the big steamers for all railroads to each railroad's specifications. Baldwin, American Locomotive (ALCo), and Lima were the biggest. It should be noted that some of the big steam engine builders converted over to manufacturing diesels and none were successful. Even though the railroads had been operating diesel-electric engines for more than ten years, these engines were used primarily for passenger trains and time freights but not in way freight service. They had also been using diesel-electric engines for yard switching.

The idea of switching from dependable, predictable steam engines to diesels with all their complexities as the backbone of freight service was pretty radical. The GP7's won them over. Since some of the southern railroads were

518 on the ground in Monona Yard at Johnson Street in the 50's

Back on the rails

Lead engine is an E8, trailing engine an E7

518 passing "518" the next afternoon

located in the middle of large, easily accessible coal fields they made the changeover to diesel-electrics a few years later, some not until the 60's. Now the coal, water towers, repair shops and other infrastructure that supported the steam engines fell into disuse. The roundhouses lasted a little longer because they would now house diesels. Later, part of the roundhouse in Madison's Monona Yard burned and the rest of it was converted to other uses.

The two biggest builders of railroad engines today are General Motor's Electro-Motive Division (EMD) and General Electric, neither of which ever built steam engines. General Electric made electrical components for other companies' diesels and then decided they could build the whole engine themselves. And they got very good at it. Fairbanks-Morse of Beloit made some diesels, most notably the Trainmaster, Baby Trainmaster, and switch engines and then they dropped out of the business. Today General Electric is the biggest builder of diesel-electric engines.

The following January, 1951, I had gotten off third shift at the depot and went home and hit the sack as usual. The next thing I remember was my cousin Graydon shaking me with some urgency and saying things like, "Get up, we've got to go up to the Navy recruiting office and sign up before they close enlistments or we're going to get drafted and we'll wind up in the Army!" Read Korea. I admired the way he had condensed the essence of his thoughts down to one concise sentence.

The Korean Conflict had started the previous June and by December had become a very hot war. It had occurred to me that my services might be requested at some point but I hadn't felt any particular urgency or even thought much about it. I was feeling some urgency now. I couldn't think of any really good argument for not going along with his obviously well-crafted plan so I climbed into my clothes and we were soon on our way uptown in his Model A roadster. I was still not very alert. No really good alternatives to his well-thought-out plan came to mind so I became resigned to all the things that were going to happen, and they did.

Two days later I was on a train to Chicago, now a revenue passenger, and thence to the Great Lakes Naval Training Center. Graydon, with all his big ideas, had to have some dental work done before he could go to boot camp so he didn't follow me until about three weeks later. The one thing that was in the back of my mind was that I was a little susceptible to motion sickness and I was joining the Navy? Oh, well. Think big ship. I would be gone for about four years. I did get a big ship, an aircraft carrier. Joining the Navy was one of the best things I ever did. Thanks in part to Graydon.

USS **Philippine Sea** *Air Group*
turning up for a strike over Korea

3

WHEN I returned to civilian life I was ready to take the next step in my plan to become a Railroad Robber Baron. I transferred into the operating department and went brakin.' I then became a member of the Brotherhood of Railroad Trainmen, one of the oldest unions in the country. My new playground for the next six years had an interesting history.

The original North Western line from Chicago to the Twin Cities was the old 19th century line through Madison and Elroy. Because it was so old it had some deficiencies such as relatively steep grades and sharp curves. Parts of it were pieces of old railroads cobbled together. The history of how railroads were developed has been described in many books, often in mind-numbing detail. Town fathers would decide that a line from their town to some other not too distant location would be to their benefit.

It could be as short as ten or fifteen miles. Bonds were sold to townsmen or whoever would buy them to finance these adventures but the money often ran out before the line was completed and these lines were often shorter than planned or were abandoned.

As more of these lines were built it became mutually advantageous for them to connect to each other to form longer, more efficient lines. Because of the lack of heavy equipment that could efficiently grade roadbeds, railroads often followed the lines of least resistance by going along existing roads or next to rivers. The line between Madison and Elroy was a combination of these smaller lines. The chronicle of the development of the Chicago and North Western from its inception in 1848 is very interesting but beyond the scope of this book.

In the early 1900's the North Western, recognizing the deficiencies of the old line through Madison, built a new line from Milwaukee through Adams to Wyeville. The geography was fairly flat and the line didn't run through any large urban areas. It was completed in 1911 and became known as the "new line" or the Adams cut-off. The Madison-Elroy line met the new line at Wyeville. Much of the old line traffic moved to this new line.

Well-financed railroads — and now we are at the Robber Baron level — built lines much more efficiently. President Lincoln was very interested in tying the nation together, ocean to ocean, with bands of steel and in 1862, during the Civil War, he authorized construction of the Union Pacific starting from the east and the Central Pacific starting from the west. The chronicle of building those railroads is very interesting. The climax of that effort was the meeting of the two railroads' tracks at Promontory Point in Utah. Who can forget the ceremony of driving the golden spike? The Great Northern was another example of an efficiently built rail line planned correctly from the start. That was the Golden Age of the Railroad Robber Barons.

Even big railroads could run out of money or interest. Later, the North Western had ambitious plans to run to the Pacific. They had a line to Casper, Wyoming, and headed west toward the Rocky Mountains. They had planned on one of three routes through the mountains, two of which could go through the Grand Tetons. They laid a track from Casper to a small town in Wyoming called Lander. Lander was basically a farm, ranch, and coal town. The depot still stands. That was the North Western's end of track to the west. The challenge of going over the Rockies may have been too *great. After you got over the Tetons you were in a large valley with another mountain range to the west. When the surveyors got to the top of the Tetons and looked west they probably said damn! and headed back to Chicago. There really wasn't much west of those mountains that would generate much revenue. The last train out of Lander was in 1976. Today on part of the road from Casper to Dubois traces of the road bed and a few very old ties can still be seen beside the highway.*

A brakeman's job was extremely dangerous in the 1800's. Engines had air brakes but railroad cars did not. Trains had to be stopped by applying the brakes on each car manually. The engine brakes usually weren't enough to stop a train.

Freight cars had a steel rod going to the roof of each car topped by a spoke wheel. Cranking the wheel applied the brakes on that car. When the train had to stop, the engineer, using his whistle, would signal the brakemen to apply the brakes. The brakemen went from car to car, setting and locking the brakes. They

Typical day on the job

had to jump the gap between cars to set the necessary number of brakes to stop the train. And there was nothing to hang onto when they landed on the next car's catwalk. They didn't have hand rails. The brakeman pictured has his lantern but is missing one important item, a club that he could insert between the spokes of the brake wheel to exert added braking pressure. Often more than two brakemen were assigned to a train depending on the grades and the number of cars in order to provide enough braking power to stop the train.

When the train was sufficiently slowed or stopped, the engineer whistled another signal telling the brakemen to release the brakes on all cars. Same deal, jumping the gap between cars and releasing the brakes. This method worked pretty well when trains were short and slow but as they got longer and heavier there were problems. Sometimes the brakemen couldn't hear the engine whistle or they misunderstood the signal. When going down grades, if the brakemen couldn't set enough brakes to slow or stop the train you had a run-away train often with disastrous consequences.

Passenger trainmen had a much easier time. The hand brakes were located in the vestibules of passenger cars so the brakemen weren't subjected to the vagaries of the weather and didn't have to jump from car to car. They could walk between cars via the vestibules. The only time I actually had to work on top of cars was on an S-shaped industrial track in Evansville with buildings built close to the track on each side. Both the point man and I had to be on the catwalks to pass signals to the engine crew.

George Westinghouse invented the air brake system for trains in the 1860's but it wasn't widely used until Congress passed a law in 1898 mandating air brakes on all rail cars. After the air brake became standard, two brakemen were usually adequate for all trains.

Another problem for the guy in the picture was coupling up cars. A link and pin system was used in those days. Basically the end of the draw bar pocket on each car was hollow and a steel link was inserted and held in place by dropping a pin through the top of the draw bar. The problem with this method was that to couple up to another car the brakeman had to guide the end of his car's link into the other car's drawbar pocket and drop the pin. Of course, one of the cars had to be moving to make the joint. This was incredibly dangerous and resulted in the loss of a lot of fingers and hands. Workers were often maimed or killed working between cars during this process. It was said that if a brakeman had all of his fingers he wasn't much of a railroader.

After I went braking, one winter night I was in the yard office waiting for the engines when a switchman walked in with a mitten that had a finger in it that wasn't his. Those kinds of injuries were still happening. About that time my engines arrived at the yard office and I was out of there. My feeling is that the Robber Barons probably never worked as brakemen or switchmen. If I had to go brakin' in those days I probably would have stuck to mail handling. But knowing that those days were all in the past I continued to pursue my dream.

I was quite familiar with the yard since I had dropped off and picked up my dad, Roger Bass, in his goings and comings on the railroad freights over the years. This switchmen's playground was a ladder style yard and they had nine tracks to work with. There were also a few other tracks, a caboose track, rip track (repair in place) for bad order cars that needed repair (their tags read BO), roundhouse lead, and so on. Switchmen not only worked in the yards but also switched the businesses and industries in the metropolitan areas that had switch yards.

Monona Yard had a large roundhouse which I had visited a few times. Once, much earlier, I went into this very large, dark, grimy building with my dad. The shop guys were putting a new tire on a driver of a steam engine. There is a lot of wear on engine driving wheels from slippage, emergency stops and just general wear and tear. The tires were steel rims three or four inches thick or more with flanges. Before they took the tires off the wheels they had to remove the drive rods. I don't know how they got the worn tires off the wheels; they probably expanded them with heat. To get the new rim on the wheel the tire was heated in a ring of fire until it was red hot. The heat expanded it so it fit on the wheel and then shrank when it cooled off. (This ring of fire may have been Johnny Cash's inspiration.) Occasionally a tire would come off on the road. The cost of a tire was way less than the cost of machining or replacing a driving wheel. Careful handling by the engineers prolonged the life of these steel tires.

There were a few other steamers in the roundhouse, some of them dead and awaiting repair and others with banked fires that were ready to go. It took five to eight hours to get a dead engine's steam up and ready to work. Hostlers worked with the engines in the yard, moving them around as necessary and performing other duties. These men were qualified to run engines in the yards but not over the road. The term hostler came from the horse-and-buggy era.

I enjoyed watching the old steam switchers chugging back and forth as the switchmen coupled up cars, backed up the engine, threw switches and kicked cars down another track to bang into a string of cars lined up on that track. They did this over and over again most of the day, breaking up incoming trains and making up new outbound trains. One of the two or three switchmen had a list of what cars went where and in what sequence. The switch lists were made up from the information the scribbler had written on his list. That was before radios so all communications were by hand signal, voice or intuition and each man seemed to know what the next move was going to be.

The engine's moves were controlled by the men on the ground; the engineer followed the switchmen's signals and the fireman kept busy shoveling coal into the red-hot firebox.

These little engines had six driving wheels and no leading or trailing trucks (0-6-0). The first M was built in 1896, M-1 in 1905. In 1917, during World War I, the United States Railroad Association mandated that for increased efficiency most steam engines would use one or two designs for each class engine. Standardized rail cars were also part of the plan. To help the war effort and the cash-strapped railroads, all of this equipment was given to them free. The North Western and its Omaha subsidiary received forty-three USRA switchers, the most of any railroad. These engines were very similar to the M-2's and the North Western's designation for them was M-3. After the government mandates were lifted in 1920 the North Western reverted to buying M-2's. The M-3's may have had too many bells and whistles, literally, for the North Western's budget. How often do you get to use that expression correctly? Both types had the same tractive effort but the M-2 was about 20,000 pounds heavier than the M-3. Some of the M's worked into the 1950's.

The picture on the next page shows the M-3 as built. Over time the North Western rebuilt tenders of some larger engines used for switching to provide better visibility for their crews. The company made a few other minor modifications to provide commonality between the M-2's and 3's. In those early days engineers were assigned their own engines. The new M-3's were well accepted by their engine crews.

John C. La Rue collection

M-2 switch engine 2150

Don Ross collection

M-3 USRA switch engine

One of the 2150's sisters, 2167, wasn't scrapped until 1952 and some worked even later. During the two weeks I worked in the yard in the summer of 1950 I don't recall seeing a steam switcher, only diesels. In discussions with engineers and switchmen of that era they said the steamers worked into the fifties in Monona Yard. The neighborhood ladies had to be pleased when those smoky old engines were finally gone since now the white sheets that they hung out to dry in the morning went back on their beds that night still white.

M-2 after Sunday wipedown

*M-3 USRA built in 1919,
in showroom condition. Sticker price $0*

4

I WAS discharged from the Navy in late 1954 and reported to the railroad and resumed my old job. I wanted to become a brakeman but business was always slow in winter so I didn't get the call until after business picked up in early spring. Another guy, Jimmy West, also wanted to go braking. He had started out as a clerk in Baraboo and worked his way up to crew caller in Madison. We both went up to the company surgeon's office for physicals. Because of the frequency of back injuries and bad knees reported by some trainmen the railroad made an extra effort to make sure that new hires for those jobs were of sound body, if not mind. The problem with those types of injuries was that it was hard to verify or disprove them and they cost the railroads significant amounts of money in claims. Also, railroads were very sensitive to lost work injuries because they had to be reported to the National Transportation Safety Board who kept score. I was put through a series of contortions that, if I didn't have a problem before, I thought I would after they finished the X-rays. I passed, Jimmy failed. He had one too many vertebra in his back. So Jimmy went back to crew calling,

Crew callers were pretty busy before the telephone came into use. Those guys had to go to the home of each railroader and give him orders for what train he was ordered for and what time to report for work. By World War II telephones were in common use. During the war railroads were given a high priority and train crewmen were given single party lines so the crew callers could always get through to call them for duty. During the war we had a private line. Most telephone lines were multiple party during that time.

I had been told that my first student run would be on the north end way freight. Way freights were trains that stopped at most stations along the way, dropping off loaded or empty cars or re-spotting loads and picking up new loads and empties. They frequently carried lumber, coal and oil, seed and fertilizer along with general freight and sometimes had an LCL (less than carload) beatup old company box car directly behind the engines. These cars carried bulky or heavy merchandise and would be spotted on the "house track" beside the freight house platform so the station agent could unload, sometimes with the help of the train crew or the customer, the John Deere cultivator or other heavy items that the locals had ordered. Some railroads had their cabooses built with doors on the sides for handling LCL. The North Western at one time had a few but I never saw one.

The railroad was near bankruptcy but I was oblivious to that. Ben Heineman had come aboard and started turning the railroad around. Somebody counted engines and found out that the railroad was almost entirely dieselized and didn't know it. Hell of a way to run a railroad! So steam engines were pulled out of service and by the end of 1956 they were almost entirely gone. In a little more than a year all but three steam engines had gone to that great roundhouse in the sky. The three engines remaining are the venerable R-1's. Make that four engines. The North Western's original, secondhand engine, the **Pioneer**, acquired in 1848, is on display in a museum in Chicago.

Hank Siles, another crew caller, called me and I was ordered to report at 7:30 for the north end way freight. Freight 563 ran from Monona Yard to Elroy, laying over and returning the next day as train 562. Hank always had a cigarette going and if you were a non-smoker, you weren't when you stopped by his office to chat. I would be going through familiar territory since I had lived in Baraboo and Reedsburg and spent time with my grandparents in Lodi and Elroy, all local stops. My grandfather had been a conductor. In a few days I would be a qualified

The Pioneer
In earlier days the pilot was called a cow-catcher.
This design apparently worked pretty well.

brakeman, sort of. Today trainmen go through months of training in the classroom and on the job to qualify.

I turned off Johnson Street onto the gravel road that went down to the Monona Yard office where train crews started and ended their runs. It was also home base for the yard switch crews, telegraphers and clerks.

I had my switch key tied to a belt loop, my time card, a lantern and a battery. The lantern had two bulbs. One had a reflector which formed a beam and the other bulb was for general area lighting and signaling. I also had a pair of leather mittens that were preferred because they were cooler and slipped on and off sweaty hands easier than gloves. My high top lace shoes that helped protect me from ankle sprains completed the picture. The yard office had the smell of old coal stoves, pipe and cigarette smoke and of working men, some trading good-natured insults as they went about their business.

Except for being taught how to couple up air hoses and opening the train line valves, you were apparently assumed by everyone to know pretty much all you needed to know about working on the railroad when you hired out or that you would soon pick it up. Or maybe it was because I was from a railroad family. Somebody may have mentioned you shouldn't ever step on the ball of the rail or run. Actually, sometimes you needed to run.

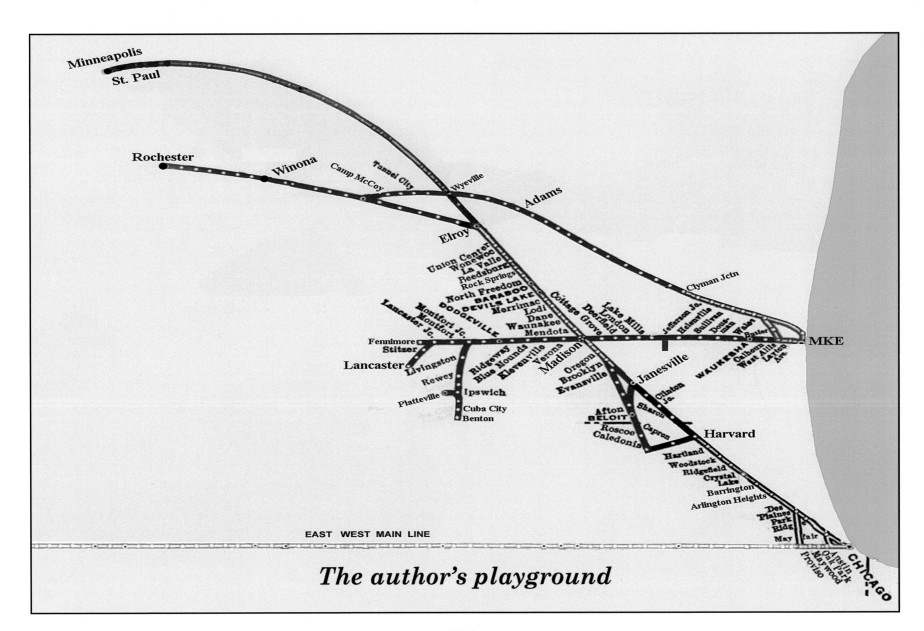

The author's playground

There were other more important things that were useful to know since ignorance could spoil your whole day. Clearances, for instance. The space between a box car and the building it services is as narrow as possible so the gap between the dock and car are at a minimum. A steel deck plate spans the gap so dollies and other equipment can go in and out of the car for loading or unloading. A clearance post is a 4 x 4 wooden post planted beside the track at the ends of buildings, painted white with **NO CLEARANCE** stenciled on it in black letters. If you were riding on a boxcar stirrup approaching one of these posts you needed to take immediate action. People usually couldn't fit between the building and the car.

I heard the engines, a low, smooth rumble, coming down the roundhouse lead and stop outside the yard office. It was a pair of GP7s, General Purpose road switchers commonly referred to as Geeps.

The head brakeman, Bob Reese, and I went out and got on the front steps of the lead engine. He signaled the fireman to back up to the next switch and stop. He opened the switch and backed the units out on the yard lead. After the engines passed through the switch he closed it and signaled the fireman to back up behind the switch that would send us down a clear track to the head of our train at the other end of the yard. He threw that switch, signaled the

GP7's

35

engineer to come ahead and we slowly moved through the yard toward the head end of our train, the engines rocking slightly from side to side on the less than perfect light yard rail. After we headed out on the west yard lead we backed through a couple switches, moving toward the head end car on our train.

When we were about three car lengths from the train Bob waved his arm three times, two times when we were two cars away, and then one wave. The engineer slowed down to a crawl. As we drifted into the car's open coupler, Bob dropped his arm.

Both knuckles closed and the pin dropped on the engine coupler. The underslung pin on the hopper dropped unseen. You couldn't see if the pin dropped on couplers with underslung pins. Then Bob raised his arm above his head and waved his hand up and down, the signal for the engineer to stretch the train. This was to make sure that the engines are coupled onto the train and that the pins on both couplers had actually dropped.

Occasionally there were instances where the engines were thought to be coupled up to the train, the train line air pumped up and the brakeman gave a highball. The engines pulled ahead without the train, losing all the air in the train line as well as the compressed air in the engine's reservoirs, which happens very quickly with a huge *whoosh*. The engineer was usually not too happy about this as he throttled up the engines to pump brand new air into his reservoirs and, after coupling up again, pumped up the train line. So far I haven't had to do anything and I'm really liking this job. Then Bob put me to work.

He showed me how to couple up the air hoses. He dropped down beside the couplers, reached under them with his left hand and grabbed the lead car's air hose which was on the far side, and with his right hand grabbed the engine hose. He swung them both up, mated them and released them. As they dropped they locked together. A successful handshake. Then he broke the coupling, stepped back and asked me to do the same. The hoses were stiff and inflexible and when I swung them up, the hose couplers were nowhere near each other. The trick was to pull back on the engine hose in my right hand, crimping it so its coupler could be easily adjusted to mate with the other hose. It was pretty simple.

The car knockers had connected the air hoses on all the cars in the train, opened all the angle cocks except the one on the back of the caboose, checked the wheel axle journal boxes for packing and lubrication and inspected the brakes and running gear. In the 50's there were very few cars with maintenance-free roller bearings. The few that had them were usually tank cars which often carried dangerously volatile liquids.

Journal box

The journal pictured clearly shows the packing but it is a sure candidate for a hotbox. It has no oil lubrication. Cars actually rode on one twenty-thousandths of an inch of oil.

On the road the crew in the engine and caboose checked the train on every curve, when the car trucks were most visible. During the day hot boxes were usually detected by tell-tale smoke. If it got hot enough there could be enough oil in the packing to catch fire and occasionally flare up the side of the car. The train would have to stop so the crew could cool down the journal with water.

At night you didn't see a hot journal until it caught fire. This was well past the smoke phase but the drill was the same. Put out the fire and move slowly to the next point where the car could be set out to be serviced later by the car men. And make sure the journal had cooled off enough. If the hot box was toward the rear of the train the caboose crew could sometimes smell the smoke. Worst case was when a hot box was not detected and the axle got so hot it burned through. Then you had some cars on the ground

Today's trains ride on highly dependable roller bearings. Further, there are heat sensors located along the tracks that can not only detect a bad bearing but report which car has the problem. Roller bearings became mandatory in 1963.

Timken roller bearings on new wheel sets

The car men were key people. They kept the cars in operating condition and repaired cars that needed attention. They could handle fairly major repairs. If a car was tagged BO, bad order, the car men were the guys that put it back into operating condition. They fixed anything from a bent stirrup to a new set of wheels. When cars broke down on the road they went to the car and took care of the problem. If there was a wreck, they took out the wreckers and picked up the pieces and put the railroad back together. Sometimes they worked around the clock to get the track back into service as quickly as possible. Today, non-railroad companies usually handle wrecks. Car knockers also watched all passing trains to make sure everything was in good order.

Bob slowly opened the angle cock, the train line valve on the engine, and the air rushed through the hoses filling the reservoirs on each car with about forty pounds of pressure. He explained that if the valve was opened too abruptly the engine air tanks would be "dynamited," that is, lose all their air. Engineers didn't like that either. Now the engineer throttled up the engines to provide more air pressure faster. Five or ten minutes later, depending on the length of the train, and after the air gauge in the caboose indicated sufficient pressure, the rear brakeman gave the signal to apply the train brakes by swinging his arm horizontally from side to side. Bob relayed the signal to the engineer to set the brakes. The engineer made a train line air reduction, which applied the brakes on all cars.

We walked toward the rear of the train checking to see that the shiny brake cylinder rod on each car was extended. When we met the rear brakeman about half way back who had checked his part of the train, Bob held his hand directly over his head which was the signal for the engineer to pump off the brakes. The increased train line air pressure forced the brake cylinder rods back into the cylinders, releasing the brake shoes from the wheels. On the way back to the head end we made sure that all the cylinder rods had retracted, checked to make sure that all the hand brakes were released, and listened for significant air leaks.

Once everyone was in position and the conductor was ready to go, the rear brakeman waved his arm over his head from side to side, giving a highball which Bob relayed to the engineer. The engineer acknowledged the signal with two blasts from the air horns which announced to everybody in the vicinity that 563 was going out of town. The people in upscale Maple Bluff, including the governor, had to love that.

The main line from Chicago to Elroy was protected by block signals. These signals gave train crews information about the track ahead.

Clear track ahead   *Redeye home signal —
Conductor call dispatcher*

The signals were on bridges or towers over or beside the tracks and usually consisted of a red arm and lights. If the arm was in the vertical position the signal light showed green which told the engine crew that the track was clear at least up to the next signal. If the arm was at a forty-five degree angle and the light showed yellow, the track was clear up to the next signal but the engineer must reduce speed and be prepared to stop at that signal because there is a train, an open switch, or a broken rail in the block beyond the signal. If the arm was horizontal there was probably something in the next block or an open switch and he must stop and then proceed with caution. To complicate this a bit, some of these signals were called home signals. These had a white bar just below the top of the arm. When the arm was in a horizontal position the train had to stop so the conductor could go to a company telephone box at the base of the signal and call the train dispatcher. The dispatcher would give specific instructions to the conductor who then informed the engineer as to what they were to do.

The conductor is the train captain. When he leaves the yard he has the waybills for every car in the train. In the course of setting out cars he leaves the waybills for those cars with the agent. Conversely, the agent gives the conductor bills for cars picked up. If the station is closed, the bills for cars that are dropped off are left in a locked box outside the depot door. The bills for cars to be picked up are left in the box by the agent for the conductor to pick up. The waybills will be sorted in train sequence when the conductor reaches the end of the run.

The engineer is responsible for safe train handling which is a very important job. With experience he learns every dip, rise and curve on the line. Many of these conditions need his special attention. Sometimes he will use only the engine brakes, known as the independent brakes, other times the train line brakes, and sometimes both. He will notch the throttle up or down depending on grades and curves and restrictive train orders. The engineer must also be totally aware of the various speed limits along the line. Everyone in the cab is supposed to call out the position of each signal when it becomes visible; "clear" for green, "forty-five" for yellow, "redeye" for horizontal. In practice, nobody called out clear unless it was the next signal after a forty-five or redeye. The color of the signal lights could not be seen in daylight.

Bob and I climbed up into the cab of the second unit, slid open the split windows on each side, pushed out the visors over the windows and flipped up the padded arm rests over the window tracks. Bob took the engineer's seat and I took the brakeman/fireman side. The engines were spooling up and we started moving forward slowly. The low rumble of the 1500 horsepower 16 cylinder 567 diesel engine moved up a pitch and the noise level increased as the train moved slowly out on the left hand west bound main over Commercial Avenue. After the caboose had cleared the yard track and got out on the main the engineer widened on the throttle. The rumble changed to a persistent, pulsating drone, setting up vibrations in the

electrical panel doors on the back bulkhead of the cab. There are eight positions or notches on the throttle. The throttle can be ratcheted up only one notch at a time because of a stop at each notch.

We were rolling out past Maple Bluff and the north end of Lake Mendota and starting up the grade toward our first stop, Mendota Mental Health Institute, a state hospital. The hopper on the head end was a load of coal for their boilers. The hospital had a gated spur so we unlocked the gate, backed the car inside the gate, set a hand brake, uncoupled, locked the gate and went back to our train.

The next stop was Waunakee, a small town like most of the rest of our stops on the way to Elroy. They usually had feed mills, lumber yards, coal yards and oil storage tanks along with various small manufacturing and canning companies. We stopped the train just before the first road crossing so we wouldn't block traffic, cut off the cars for the town and pulled up to the depot where the station agent, conductor and rear brakeman would discuss where the cars were to be spotted and what loads or empties we were to pick up or re-spot. Each town had a depot and a station agent/telegrapher. They represented the railroad's interests, handling damage claims, working with the local businesses to provide for all their transportation needs, and generally giving them good customer service. The agent also had to be a diplomat. "Where's the shipment you promised me two days ago?" "I'm filing a claim for damages on the load of furniture I got yesterday!" Often the difference between businesses choosing train versus truck was which one gave the best price within an acceptable time frame. Bulk commodities like lumber, coal, and fuel oil almost always moved by rail. The worse thing about the agent's job during WWII was delivering the telegrams:

`"THE WAR DEPARTMENT REGRETS`
`    TO INFORM YOU . . . "`

After we had finished the work we left Waunakee and headed up the hill to Dane, the smallest town between Madison and Reedsburg. This hill had a relatively steep grade. The engineer had the throttle in run 8. The controlling grade between Madison and Elroy was between Madison and Baraboo and was either the grade up to Dane or the grade up through the Baraboo Hills. The employee time table showed how much tonnage each class of engine could pull up the hill. For instance, for this grade a GP7 could pull 1,950 tons up the hill compared to the 2,100 tons a Mikado steam engine could handle. The north end way freight normally ran with two Geeps, so tonnage was not usually a factor.

We probably passed through Dane without stopping, going down the other side of the hill and around a right hand curve into Lodi which had a canning company and probably still does today. Farmers brought their produce to town to be processed and canned locally and the finished product was shipped out by rail. One day in late summer we were switching them out and they were canning corn. One of the workers got an empty bucket, threw in some ears of corn, husks and all, and sprayed them with live steam. They came out very hot and very good. (Many years later technology finally caught up — instead of using a bucket and live steam, the microwave oven became the instrument of choice, along with instructions as to how to get the best and most consistent results. Five minutes for one ear and one more minute for each additional ear and you get the same results as a steamed bucket full of sweet corn but without the drama. Butter and season to taste. The bucket and live steam method was much faster and more exciting).

I was hanging pretty close to Bob and watched what he and the other brakeman were doing. In the course of switching we were moving back and forth over street crossings. The conductor usually, but not always, guarded the street crossings during those back and forth movements. The head brakeman stayed with the engines, watching for signals from his partner who had the switch list. After the switching was finished, empties or recently loaded cars were added to the train or set out on a side track to be picked up by our opposite freight, today's eastbound 562, or by us on our return trip to Madison the next day. A secure hand brake was set on these cars to make sure they didn't roll out and foul the main line.

To protect the main line there is usually a bright yellow derailer in place on one rail of all side tracks that lead to the main. These are small steel devices that are hinged. They usually lie flat on the ball of one of the rails. When a train goes into or out of a track on the main line the brakeman unlocks and flips the derailer so that it lies flat beside the rail. When it is in the derail position on top of the track, the flange on the wheel of the lead truck on a wayward car will ride up the groove in the derailer and force the wheel over the rail, putting the car on the ground. The derail was on the farthest rail from the main line so it diverted the wayward car off the track away from the main. Some derails were connected by a pipe to the switch stand, which then had to do double duty. When the switch was opened it flipped the derailer off the track. When the switch was closed the derailer flopped back on the ball of the rail, protecting the main. To move the switch points and flip the derailer the brakeman usually had to pull back pretty hard on the switch handle. Derailers that weren't pipe connected were locked.

Derail protecting the main line

When switching cars, the air in the air brake reservoir is usually bled off so the cars will roll freely. If these cars are left on a siding the brakeman will either set the hand brake on the car or chip a wheel. A surprisingly small stick of wood works well if it is placed in front of the wheel at the instant the car stops. If the car starts to roll forward before the chip is in place it will often roll over the chip. In another situation a brakeman may make a setout, that is, back a car with a full reservoir into a siding and uncouple it from the train. When the air

hose uncouples, the air in the brake cylinders will set the brakes, securing the car. Over time, the reservoir slowly loses its air and if a hand brake wasn't set or a wheel chipped, the car could roll one way or the other. A strong wind could move a box car that's not secured, or if the siding wasn't flat it could roll out towards the main and you hope the derail will do its job. A perfectly round wheel on a perfectly flat surface with almost no friction involved will roll very easily. A standing rail car can roll on a 0.7 percent grade. And these rolling cars are completely silent. More than once in a dark yard I would be aware of a huge black shadow silently rolling by and you think what if . . .

Going out of Lodi we passed Okee, which has a store and a couple of houses, heading for the big bridge over the Wisconsin River at Merrimac. Highway 113 and Okee are separated by a railroad grade cut, with resulting berms between the tracks and the small Okee store on one side and highway 113 on the other. The track made a long curve to the left and as it approached the bridge it curved right.

Our family had crossed the river on the Merrimac Ferry many times going to Baraboo, Reedsburg, or Devil's Lake. The ferry connected Sauk and Columbia counties. It gave a great panoramic view of the bridge and on a good day we might be lucky enough to see a train going over it. The bridge was about a third of a mile long and the structure is not symmetrical. One day I noticed that the center portion was actually a swing bridge. It rotated ninety degrees when opened so boats could pass. In earlier days a swing bridge was called a draw bridge. Classic Mississippi steam boats had used this portion of the river but their days had come to an end and the bridge probably hadn't opened after the mid-1920's.

Merrimac Bridge looking
west from engine cab

The view out the engine cab window is now a grand vista. As you round the curve and head out over the bridge the ground falls away and you are suddenly very high up in the air with nothing but two thin bands of bright steel that fade to brown against a background of narrowing brown ties between you and the river. Worse, there is now a very hollow empty sound under the engine trucks. The nose of the engine which had seemed proportional to the tracks ahead now seemed way too wide for the bridge. Train speed over the bridge was restricted to 20 miles per hour so it was a leisurely ride to the other side, until once again we heard the comforting sound of the trucks on solid ground.

An old time engineer told me that when he was a young fireman an old, old time engineer told him never to set the brakes on a train on the bridge. He was told that the footings weren't in very good shape and by setting the brakes the bridge would be dragged in the same direction as the train with predictable results. I'm glad I never had to pull the air on the bridge. Or did they get the footings fixed by the 50's?

3 F7's crossing the Wisconsin River on the Merrimac Bridge

After the engineer estimated that the caboose was off the bridge he widened on the throttle urging his three thousand ponies up the long grade toward the Baraboo Hills. From here past the bluffs and Devil's Lake to Baraboo is the most scenic part of the run. As you entered the heavily wooded bluffs there was a not very active quarry owned by the state of Wisconsin. Occasionally we would drop off or pick up ore cars and take them to Baraboo or Madison. This quarry was normally switched by the Baraboo switch crew. These cars loaded were very heavy and had short wheel bases which made them unstable so when they were in the consist* trains ran at restricted speed.

As we approached the South Shore the engineer started whistling frequently. Rather than climb the bluffs to get from one shore to the other, people often walked the tracks which was a lot easier. Some trails crossed the tracks and tourists needed to be warned. If there were a lot of people on the tracks, as we approached, they casually moved off the roadbed like the parting of the waters. There was an occasional young man that was more deliberate then the others, probably on his first outing trying to impress his lady of the moment. The crew watched with a little more intensity then usual through this area, pretty sure that nothing would happen but there was still the bend around the bluff that will take us along the lakeshore of Devil's Lake and more tourists ahead.

The trackage between Lodi and Baraboo may be some of the most scenic on the North Western system. Past Lodi the track runs beside Lake Wisconsin. Just past Okee the track curves to the right and goes over a high bridge a third of a mile long and then curves to the left. A short distance later another curve to the right and it's up into the beautiful Baraboo hills. In the fall when the leaves change color this is an incredible sight. At the top of the hill the roadbed flattens out as it goes into Devil's Lake State Park. Another curve to the right and the track runs between the east bluff and the pristine Devil's Lake on the left. Across the lake the west bluff drops down to meet the other shore. You're now in a different world.

* consist = all cars in a train except the locomotive.

Too bad only an engineer and conductor can now enjoy this sight.

I had an interesting experience on the stretch of track beside the lake in the 40's. Our Boy Scout troop was camping on the South Shore of the lake and we had hiked toward the North Shore along the roadbed. We saw a long telephone pole in the water and decided to take it to the South Shore swimming area. We started out pushing it ahead of us as we swam. It was pretty slow going so we figured the best way to get it to the South Shore was to lay it across the rails and drag it. It was very wet, waterlogged and heavy and should slide down the rails real good. We tied a rope on each end and started dragging it crosswise down the rails. I knew passenger train 501 was due mid-afternoon. It was actually scheduled to pass Devil's Lake at 3:16. I told the guys that we should pull our prize down the eastbound main and 501 would pass on the westbound main, no problem.

We heard her whistling and watched as she came steaming around the bend from South Shore and along the lake. It was a gorgeous but terrifying sight. She had a full head of steam as she came flat out through Devil's Lake Park. She was on the eastbound main! Panic! I'm the big railroad expert and felt a huge sense of responsibility. Some guys froze. I and a couple other guys grabbed the end of the pole between the mains and horsed it over to the bluff side of the roadbed. The train blew by and I don't know if the engineer set the brakes. I know he couldn't have stopped. When they stopped at the depot in Baraboo I'm sure the engineer called the train dispatcher and reported that a bunch of damn fool kids were dragging a telephone pole down his tracks beside the lake! To this day I can't figure out why the train was on the eastbound main or what would have happened if the engine hit the pole. I guess I also owe the engine crew a long overdue apology.

Our next stop was Baraboo, the biggest town on the run. It had a fair-sized switch yard and an abandoned roundhouse, then being used as a scrapyard by a local businessman. The depot was a large two-story masonry structure and was quite handsome, built in the early

Baraboo Depot. No platform cover, no order boards. Almost no trains. Roadrailers sit idly on a side track.

Madison to Lancaster and beyond on the West End. Over time that line became shorter and shorter.

The Baraboo yard had a steam engine for switching out the yard and servicing local businesses. This engine, a Class R-1, was a big step up in size and power for the North Western when it was introduced in 1901 and caused a great deal of excitement among businessmen and townsmen alike along the line. Its wheel arrangement was 4-6-0, known as a ten-wheeler. It was larger and heavier then any other North Western engines at the time and the railroad had to beef up bridges and widen trackside and overhead clearances to accommodate it. The engines were quite impressive compared to the other engines the North Western had at the time. The engine roundhouse stalls at Baraboo and other yards had to be extended and turntables lengthened to accommodate them.

1900's. It had the usual separate men's and women's waiting rooms. In the early years Baraboo had a large roundhouse and various shops to maintain and repair equipment. Many hundreds of railroad men lived in Baraboo. Some say that about half the townsmen worked for the North Western. At one time it had been the headquarters for the Madison Division, controlling the tracks from Harvard, Illinois, to Elroy, from Madison to Milwaukee, and

R-1 894 switching the Baraboo yard.
Baraboo depot in the background.

R-1 894 switching the Baraboo yard mid-50's

After finishing our work in Baraboo, we parked the train and one of the crewmen passed the universally understood hand signal to the rest of the crew, closed fists moving alternately up and down toward the mouth. Time to eat. Railroad crews usually knew where the best "greasy spoons" were that were available in the wide lunchtime window they had. We walked a block down the hill from the Baraboo depot to a small, very nice restaurant. The fireman would have set the hand brake on one of the engines and the engineer pulled the reversing lever out of the control stand and put it in his pocket. The engines were left running but without the reversing lever they could not be moved. Train crews were pretty conscientious about eating and getting back on the job. The stores on the block that housed the restaurant are now all empty.

It seemed that often the engine crew sat by themselves. There may have been a number of reasons for this. There was less turnover among engineers and they probably knew each other better. They were also more technically trained and were responsible for very large complicated pieces of equipment and therefore had more in common with each other. Or could it have been that there just wasn't enough room for five at the table? Trainmen required less technical knowledge. There also seemed to be a gap between trainmen and yard switchmen who both used the same yard office. The switchmen probably worked harder than road crews because they were on the ground switching more of the time. Trainmen spent a fair amount of time riding the trains but at least the switchmen got to go home at the end of their shifts. And the switchmen had a little known added benefit. Sometimes the ladies whose back yards bordered on the rail yard forgot to pull down their shades at night.

After lunch we got back on the train and headed out to North Freedom, the location of some old, never very profitable iron mines and clay red from iron that was used for a time by the North Western for paint coloring. The spur was about four or five miles long back to the mines and crossed one highway that had a bar and restaurant, place named La Rue. We stopped at the switch to La Rue, cut off the two GP7's we always used on that job and backed in to make a pick-up. In a matter of minutes we went from 79 mile an hour main line rail to less than 10 mile an hour rail at best, a giant step back into the past. The track was probably 65 pound rail* and the ties, at least those that could be seen, had faded to a dusty brown color.

On the back end of the engines my partner and I had a very good view of the weed-choked sunken roadbed. Were we going to make it? Obviously the guys that had spotted the car we were going to pick up did. Fortunately for the engine crew on the head end they couldn't see the track they were backing in on. At least not on the way in. I thought every trip to La Rue was going to be my last down that line. Little did I know that a few years later it would be the main line of a new, up-and-coming railroad!

*Traditionally, rail is rated in pounds per yard.

We had been running on the future engine house track of the Mid-Continent Railroad Museum. Now I have to buy a ticket to ride. Who'd a thought?

The next town was Rock Springs, a small non-descript town formerly named Abelmans. In the 40's our family lived in a place outside of Reedsburg and we often had to take dad down to the Baraboo depot to deadhead to Elroy or Madison to his next job. And to pick him up when he deadheaded back. There was a flagman

Paul Swanson colleciton

Work train at Rock Springs, probably a weed sprayer. The depot was later moved to the Midcontinent Railroad Museum grounds and restored.

at the crossing (he also had a little house like the one in Madison) who carefully cultivated a colorful flower garden.

In the late 50's a quarry called the Pink Lady was started there. The pink quartzite that they mined and crushed there was used, among other things, as ballast on the North Western and other railroads' road beds. That stone was very hard with sharp edges. The railroad liked it because it packed tightly and held the ties firmly in place, keeping the rails in alignment. Strangely, after the Union Pacific bought the North Western in 1995 they discontinued the use of pink lady ballast on their railroad. They said it was so sharp that it tore up their ties. Later they started using it. On some new trackage, railroads are installing concrete ties. They will last a lot longer than the old creosoted wood ties which are still very much in use today. The Rock Springs depot, or what was left of it, was moved to the Mid-Continent museum grounds and restored. The Pink Lady quarry is still in operation.

The next stop, Reedsburg, was the second biggest town on the line but required the most switching. Baraboo was the biggest but they had a switch crew working full time doing the switching chores, at least until 1957. Reedsburg sometimes presented a pretty good challenge for the brakeman carrying the list. Occasionally there was so much work on the north end way freight that an extra brakeman, a swing man, was assigned to the regular crew. He, the conductor and the station agent would get together and discuss what needed to be done for the day. The Reedsburg depot still stands today and is in very nice shape. It had been designed with a ladies' waiting room but the docents there don't seem to know that.

There is no one right way to switch out a town with a lot of businesses and cars to handle. Every brakeman would do it a different way, some better, some not as good. Like chess, a good brakeman planned his work two or three moves ahead. Some men were better at it or more experienced than others. I don't know if guys think about it but I think the rest of the crew was aware, in a non-judgmental way, what kind of a job the man with the list was doing.

There's a saying, every move a picture. I really liked that one. That was probably not verbalized if a man was doing a good job but could be used occasionally, tongue in cheek, if he made a mistake and knew it. I think most trainmen knew where they stood in terms of their switching ability compared to the other men. Like any other group, they probably had opinions about the other guys, either ability- or personality-wise. Railroad men were usually pretty tolerant of each other even though not everybody was a winner. But it did take awhile to learn the ins and outs of all the tracks, towns and industries on the division.

There isn't much to say about the next three small towns. Nothing very remarkable about LaValle except that in the 40's Dad took the family over there from where we were living in an old log cabin during the summer near Reedsburg to see an outdoor movie before there were outdoor movies. Somebody set up a screen and projector in the park and most everybody sat on the ground watching the movie. It even had sound and some people watched from their cars. This was obviously a town way ahead of its time. Popcorn wasn't served but much later somebody somewhere finally got that right. Was this the birth of the drive-in theater?

Wonewoc had an active Ray-O-Vac battery manufacturing plant. We brought in some of the makings and took out the finished batteries. Union Center had a Carnation Milk plant producing the retail cans of condensed milk you still see on your grocer's shelves. Our last stop was Elroy, four miles away.

Elroy was the interface between the C&NW and The Chicago, St. Paul, Minneapolis and Omaha railroad, commonly known as the Omaha. It was a wholly owned subsidiary of the Chicago and North Western but operated independently under its own management. Much of their equipment, engines and cars and so on, were about the same design as the C&NW's. The early Omaha steam engines usually mounted their headlights over the smoke box ahead of the stack. The North Western mounted theirs in front of the smoke box. This little known fact is useful to know if you ever see a real old steam engine that could have been an Omaha or North Western engine. Who knows why they were different? Another difference was the caboose windows. The North Western used barn windows with four individual panes in each window. The Omaha windows were all single pane. Their Elroy rail yard was not very active then but it did have a round-house and in earlier years had been a very active facility. I wish I had walked over and looked over some of their remaining steamers. And better yet, taken a camera.

The North Western depot at Elroy was a big old red wooden building with a covered platform and still stands today. It had a restaurant because in those days there were quite a few passengers changing trains and they had time to grab some food before the next leg of their journey. The restaurant, complete with hanging fly paper, was on its last legs and finally closed sometime in the later fifties. Big Al was the proprietor with a white slightly stained apron and rolled up sleeves. He looked pretty much like the picture you now have of him in your mind's eye. He was a good ol' boy.

Tom Wilson

Passenger train at Elroy pulled by E-2 2901 between the depot and hotel, mid-50's

Elroy depot with hotel in background, about 1980

I'm told that today the depot houses the Elroy fire department.

There was a side track beside the main line across from the depot that could hold about twenty cars. If our train fit on it, and it usually could, we tied up on that track. If we had more cars than that track could hold we had to take our train into the Omaha yards, for which we got extra pay. On more than one day we were close to the limit and we intentionally picked up an extra car at Union Center forcing us into the Omaha yard. Was that featherbedding? Nah.

The maximum time that could be worked at one stretch was sixteen hours. If you couldn't get your train into a yard by then you died on the road. The train had to stop, the dispatcher was called and a relief crew was sent out to bring your train into the yard. The regular crew were just passengers. That never happened to me but I remember at least two sixteen hour days. When you tied up after sixteen hours you were really dragging and you remembered those days. A lot of getting on and off cars, climbing ladders to the top and down the other end to get to the hand brakes, walking back and forth between switches and on and on. And the heat didn't help. When you were really fatigued is when bad things could happen so you had to really concentrate on what you were doing. And we were working in the dark towards the end of our day. Both of those long days were at Union Center with four miles to go. Today the maximum day is twelve hours. On one trip we tied up with minutes to spare. Another trip, which I clearly remember, we didn't quite make it in sixteen hours but the train register showed sixteen hours, thanks to an operator/telegrapher who wasn't a clock watcher. You didn't read that here.

The crews on 563 usually did not sleep in the caboose. There may have been bunks on the second floor of the depot but I didn't carry a bed roll and went over to the old hotel on the other side of the tracks for the night. I think it cost two bucks a night but you only live once. In the even earlier times this was the place where traveling salesmen and probably a few passengers spent the night. The rooms were small and very well kept. There was the standard sink in each room and the facilities were down the hall. This hotel was the prototypical depot hotel of the early 1900's and still stands today, a very nice looking hotel.

After we tied up we got supper and some of the guys went up to the main street a block away and spent the evening in one of the local saloons. What else was there to do? I usually hung around the depot, saving myself for the bright lights of State Street in Madison the next night. Later there was often a card game going on in a small, smoky room in the west end of the depot. Or so I'm told. Complex, competitive games like poker are said to keep the mind sharp and these guys had sharp minds.

Railroaders, like traveling salesmen, had a lot of time away from home and were left to their own devices for passing the time away. Some guys found companionship. One brakeman had a wife at one end of his run and a lady friend at the other. One night he had a heart attack and died suddenly, at the wrong end of his run.

The departure time for the return trip to Monona yard was about 8:30 the next morning. We had done most of the switching on the westbound trip the previous day so today would be a much shorter, easier day. We mostly did some re-spots and picked up loads and empties we'd left on side tracks or that the opposite train crew had switched out for us to pick up on the way back to Madison. Sometimes this meant we had a fairly heavy train.

The only time I had to double a hill was on 562 going up the grade out of Lodi to Dane. This was the eastbound controlling grade. Occasionally in the course of dropping off and picking up cars you reached or exceeded the pulling capacity of your power. The conductor kept track of cars in the train but in the course of picking up and dropping off cars nobody knew for sure what the actual tonnage of the train was. And sometimes the engines weren't having a good day. When we were about a quarter of a mile from the top of the hill we gradually slowed to a stop. For power we had the usual two GP7's which are each rated at 1500 horsepower and each could pull 1,950 tons up any grade between Elroy and Madison. We obviously had a train that weighed more than 3,900 tons or one or both engines weren't operating at their rated capacity. The GP7 redlines at 825 amperes but could be operated at higher amperage for a specifically defined period of time, about five minutes, before bad things start to happen, like burning out the traction motors. And engineers just hated that and so did the Company. We reached those limits so we had to double the hill.

Doubling a hill simply means you take your train over the top of the hill in two pieces. A brakeman cuts off part of the train which is then taken to the first siding over the hill and parked. The engines come back and pull the back end of the train up and leave it on the main line beside the first cut. To keep the train in sequence and the caboose on the back end, the engines grab the cars on the siding, couple them onto the end of the train sitting on the main and proceed. The next town before Madison was Waunakee and we probably didn't stop there or if we did there wasn't much to do. Sometimes we had to go in the siding there to let the Dakota 400 pass.

One day there was a terrible accident at the grade crossing just east of the Waunakee siding. Dad was the conductor on 562 and they had taken the siding at Waunakee to clear the main for the Dakota 400. Dad's freight was standing quite a ways west of the road. The crossing was protected by flashing lights and bells and 562 was far enough back so the crossing signals weren't activated by its engines.

Way freight 562 in the hole for the Dakota 400, powered by an E8 and E7 at Waunakee.
Two Geeps head up the way freight. The old wood company box car behind the engines
is the LCL car. The farmer on the grade crossing had about ten seconds to live.
On another day the 400, also headed by an E8 and E7, sideswiped a switch engine in Monona Yard.
Note that by now the North Western had gone from engine wiping to engine washing.

A farmer on a tractor was approaching the crossing from the north. As the 400 approached, the signals went on. The 400 was on the other side of the way freight and wasn't visible to the farmer until it passed 562's engines. The 400 was whistling the crossing but the farmer probably couldn't hear it over the sound of his tractor and obviously thought the signals were activated by the way freight and he had plenty of time to get across. When he saw the stream-liner it was too late. He did not survive.

The farmer's house was on the southeast corner of the intersection. A short time later I was on 563 and when we whistled that crossing a little boy about three years old came running over to the edge of his yard waving to us. His mother came running out of the house, grabbed him by the arm and hustled him back to the house. He had no idea what was going on. It was a very sad moment. That incident has always stuck in my mind and I still remember it very clearly. Today only the basement with a tub at the bottom remains on the property.

From Waunakee to Monona Yard is pretty much downhill and fast track. We hit the yard limit board and headed into a clear track and yarded the train. I cut the engines off and sent them down the house lead to the roundhouse. By this time the conductor would have completed his wheel report, a list of every car in the train showing the car's initials, number, contents, destination and weight. The conductor and rear brakeman walked up from the caboose to the yard office where the conductor dropped off the way bills, wheel report, pay slips and company mail, entered the time tied up and signed the register. It starts all over the next morning, six days a week for this train.

5

A NORTH WESTERN
conductor's wife invented the Kromer cap
which was widely used by railroad men in the
winter. It was made of wool, very warm and had
a band that could be pulled down over the ears
in especially bad weather. She had cobbled
something up and with added improvements
came up with a serviceable cap which has with-
stood the test of time. She should have gotten an
honorary *Employee of the Month Award*. The cap
was like Henry Ford's Model T, you could get it
in any color you wanted as long as it was black.
The Kromer company was sold a few years ago
but the cap is still available, now in colors.

Roger, Charles, and Ben Bass

61

My grandfather, Ben Bass, began his career in 1907 as an engine wiper in the Baraboo roundhouse. I'm not sure if his goal was to become a Railroad Robber Baron and like me, he also started at the bottom of the ladder and became a conductor. He spent forty-four years on the railroad.

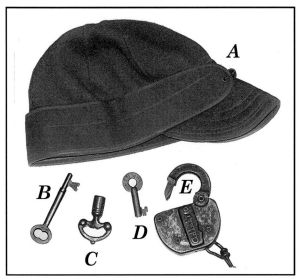

A. *Kromer cap*   B. *Coach key*
C. *Gas light key*   D. *Switch key*
E. *Standard North Western lock*

The Madison Division crews worked the Adams cut-off, also known as the new line, which ran from Milwaukee to Wyeville, where it met the old line west of Elroy. This track was completed in 1911. Most time freight traffic went to the new line but there were a few way freights. Ben worked out of Adams for a while and probably worked the queen of them all, the 400. As time went by other streamlined trains were called 400 and were given unique names such as the Dakota 400 and the Flambeau 400. The original 400 became the Twin Cities 400.

My father, Roger, started out on the signal gang in 1929. Shortly after, he moved over into the operating department as a brakeman. Soon thereafter he was laid off. It had something to do with an economic crunch about that time. He was finally called back in 1936 but the railroad still wasn't doing too well so he couldn't hold a regular job. Ben was well established during that period and was never laid off. He provided financial support for our family and apparently we never went on welfare. The economy didn't start to come back until 1940 with a war looming and then business boomed. Roosevelt provided some programs like the Civilian Conservation Corps and the WPA that helped ease the economic pain for a lot of people from 1932 to 1940. Dad's years on the C&NW roster were from 1929 to 1971, forty-two years. I don't think he aspired to become a Railroad Robber Baron.

I hired out in 1950 so my time on the roster was eleven years, but like dad, not all of those years were worked. You had to work at least once a month for that month to be counted as a month worked toward railroad retirement. If you worked 120 months you earned a railroad retirement benefit. If you worked fewer months than that your railroad retirement benefits were rolled into Social Security. That's what happened in my case. I was on the roster for eleven years but did not work 120 months. The total time the three of us were on the North Western roster was 97 years.

I don't think I ever read the book of rules cover to cover. Trainmen were periodically given a test on the rules but I don't recall ever being asked to take one. But I do have a Certificate of Examination card, number 27107, that says I was tested on August 1, 1957, and passed. One of these days I'm going to read the book

to see what I missed. Probably a lot. I did get a physical every year except 1960 and 1961.

Some conductors' tools of the trade

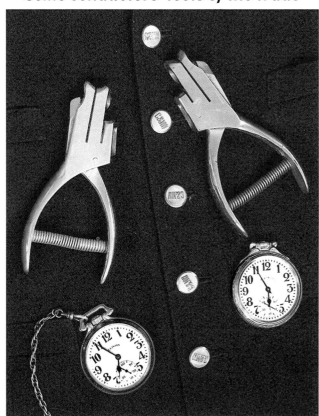

Ben's punch and gold watch on left, Roger's punch and silver watch on right. Background is Roger's passenger uniform vest. Both watches are Illinois brand.

I was conscious of the fact that I had to do a better than average job. I was the son of Roger Bass and wanted to make sure he never heard any negative comments about my work.

The GP7 was classified as a road switcher. It was longer than the yard switchers, with a short extended hood ahead of the cab and had trucks and axles geared to much higher speeds.

The early units came with foot boards on each end of the engine instead of pilots making switching with them much easier for the brakemen than with covered wagons* or steam engines. Later the foot boards would give way to small snow plows which worked well in the upper Midwest.

*Engines streamlined with shrouding

The Chicago & North Western received the first GP7's built by GM's Electro-Motive Division

Engine crew visibility was also much better on these diesels than on steam engines or covered wagons. They were good riders and much more comfortable engines. They were powered by a sixteen cylinder diesel engine, designated 567, connected to an electrical generator that powered the drive motors, one motor on each of the four axles, and they were very dependable.

The GP7 demonstrators that I saw in the fall of 1950 pulling 594 were purchased by the North Western. They had been operating for a few months as demonstrators on various railroads and, as I recall, were painted in a blue color with white trim. When the North Western bought them they numbered them 1518, 1519, and 1520. In 1950 I never imagined that one day I would be sitting in one of those units on the head of that same train, eastbound for Proviso Yard. The 1518 was donated to the Illinois Railroad Museum by the North Western.

The ALCo RS-3's were similarly configured and with a bit more horsepower. These engines had been introduced a few years before the

Two Geeps heading up a freight approaching Blair Street

GP7's. They were supercharged and when they accelerated would emit a large cloud of black smoke similar to a steamer's. I caught a job on one and it didn't match up with Geeps very well as far as comfort. I think it had a wood floor and was a hard rider. It had better acceleration than the Geep but always looked black and grimy.

These engines eventually gravitated to northern Wisconsin and west to the Omaha line, a wholly owned subsidiary of the C&NW, and served out there very capably.

North Western and most other railroads that used these ALCo engines ran with the long

ALCo RS-3

end forward. I've asked engineers why they did that and nobody seems to know. The thinking may have been that, like steam engines, it provided more protection for the engine crew. Or was it because that's the way engines should run? Some were equipped with dual controls so they could operate normally in either direction.

They were the first of a new class of freight engines that would have a major impact on the railroad industry. Streamlined diesel-electric engines, usually class E's built by what was then the General Motors Electro-Motive Division, came into service in the late 30's

pulling passengers trains. These engines had two sets of motor-generators, each putting out about 1000 horsepower and were used exclusively for passenger service. The first of these engines, type E3, had a long, sloping, very graceful-looking nose. This design was used through the E6 models. Later units had a little more power.

These engines were followed in the mid-40's by a freight version, designated F, units a little shorter but of the same basic design and with only one motor/generator set. The nose of the F units was changed from the earlier design

EMD Passenger E7's

67

of the sloping E's. The F's had a more vertical nose, referred to as a bulldog nose. The next E units, E7, 8 and 9, also received the bulldog nose.

The F's were rated at 1,500 horsepower. The first of these engines sold in quantity were designated FA's, followed by F3's, F7's and F9's. All engines of this design were generically referred to as covered wagons by railroaders. The freight version was used mostly on time freights, trains that ran from point to point with few stops in between. These engines did not work well in way freight work. There was no good place on the front end of the engine for the brakeman to ride in the course of his switching duties and the engine crew's field of vision was limited.

With the introduction of diesel-electric freight engines there were labor considerations that had to be resolved. All steam engines had

EMD Passenger E8's

to have an engineer and a fireman for obvious reasons, so a double-headed freight, that is, two steam engines, had a two-man crew for each engine. With the new diesels one engine crew could operate multiple units. The units were electrically cabled to each other and all units responded to the engineer's actions in the lead unit. They were referred to as m.u.'s, multiple units. The Brotherhood of Railroad Engineers felt that to protect their jobs, each unit with a cab had to have an engine crew even though they weren't needed. They were simply non-revenue passengers. Some may have suggested this was feather-bedding.

To get around this problem some railroads ordered their freight units in sets of three, permanently connected together, the front unit A, with a cab, the middle unit B, blind on both ends, and the rear unit C, also a cab unit.

EMD Freight F3's

69

EMD Freight F7's

These three units were then defined as a single engine that would require only one crew. That solved the crewing problem but in the grand scheme of things, it didn't work very well for the railroads. There was the Law of Unintended Consequences thing. When one of the three units needed repair or maintenance the other two perfectly serviceable units were also out of service, becoming little more than two very large paperweights. It was back to the bargaining table and things got worked out. Now these units could be used in any combination with one engine crew, the lead unit of course always being a cab unit.

6

O**F ALL** the North Western
steam engines, Class R-1 lasted the longest.
They were produced from 1901 to 1908.
Class D, which was first built a year earlier
than the R-1's, was retired earlier than them.
The 894 that switched the Baraboo yards in
1955 was built in 1907 and may have been the
last steam engine on the Madison district. The
R-1 that worked there was replaced by a diesel
in 1956 and the diesel itself was eliminated in
1957. The north end way freight took over the
Baraboo switching duties in 1957.

From its introduction, the R-1 was the
railroad's main line freight engine and, along
with the D's, served as a passenger engine.
After bigger engines were introduced it served
on secondary lines for many years thereafter.

It was very capable doing either job. As time went on more powerful engines were introduced and the R-1's were relegated to branch line service. Many of the branch lines were not upgraded to handle newer, heavier engines. Some R-1's were also relegated to switching service and their tenders were modified to provide better visibility between the engine crew and the switchmen. The tender on 894 is a good example of the changes that were made for switching service. The coal hopper was narrowed and built higher to carry about the same amount of coal as it could before. The pictures of 894 clearly show the difference and the improved visibility [p.50].

There are three R-1's left in the country, none in operating condition. The Mid-Continent Railroad Museum has one that is in storage waiting to be restored and put back into service. Its number is 1385 and it has had a storied career since it joined the museum in 1963. It had been put back into operating condition by museum volunteers and used for many years to pull tourist trains on an old spur that ran from North Freedom to La Rue. It also toured the system under the sponsorship of the Chicago & North Western Railway. Since it will cost almost

1385 at work

a million dollars to restore and meet today's safety standards it won't steam again for a long time. It is the longest-lived North Western engine.

Engine 1385, at present in storage at the Mid-Continent Railroad Museum, was also built in 1907. Coincidentally that was the year my grandfather went to work on the North Western as an engine wiper in Baraboo. Ben Bass was a fiddle player in rural Sauk County and at age 25 decided he needed a real job. He had married Nellie Bates the year before and had a child on the way who was to become my father. Engine wiping wasn't much of a job. It probably had a five-minute learning curve and required a lot of elbow grease. It was an entry level position but he worked his way up and retired as a conductor in 1951. Along with the building of 1385 and 894 and Ben getting a job and the birth of my father, Roger Bass, 1907 was indeed a very good year.

1385 in action

After the switching job was eliminated, the north end way freight handled the Baraboo switching duties. One year after the switch engines were eliminated we had to weigh a number of outbound loads. The scale was too short to hold the whole car, cars had gotten longer over time, so we had to weigh each end

73

separately and add the two together and we had to do it the hard way. We didn't have calculators in those days.

One day in January we had to do some switching at Baraboo. We had a cold spell and I dressed for worst case weather. Dad had purchased a WW II flight suit used by crews of high-flying strategic bombers, B-17's and B-24's. It was a clear, bitter cold day and I wore the suit, bulky as it was. It probably worked well

1385 taking on water

1385 restored, above . . .

for the waist gunners on a B-17 but if you had to walk around in it, it was pretty clumsy. The gunners didn't have to walk though they probably would have preferred to. I was riding the point on a shove to the west end of the yard and got the full effect of a brisk westerly wind. The thermometer outside the operator's shack read 24 below. Those were the kinds of days you really wanted to be working in the freight house or even sweeping the depot.

I had the opportunity to work on a job with an R-1 in 1955 or '56. Dad and I took a work train to the tunnels north of Elroy. Our job was to dig out sediment that had washed down beside the mouths of the tunnels. It was one of only a couple of times we caught the same job. Behind the engine there was a gondola for sediment, a track mounted shovel, another gondola for sediment and the caboose. Our power was an R-1, one of the 3700's, and it was

the only steam engine I ever worked on. I regret that I rode the caboose with dad and the rear brakeman rather than ride the engine. These three tunnels are now part of a very popular hiking and biking trail, the 400 Trail.

. . . and as it looked in 2007

75

Work train, Elroy tunnels —
Left to right: Roger Bass, conductor;
Ted Barcio, roadmaster; Elmer Ebert, flagman

Work train, Elroy tunnels

Conductor Roger Bass, third from right

Work train, Elroy tunnels

The Class Z Consolidation was the next engine purchased after the R-1's. This engine had a wheel arrangement of 2-8-0 and was quite powerful. The R-1's production ended in 1908 and the Zulu was produced from 1909 to 1913. Two hundred fifty were built. They worked into the 50's. In 1913 the Mikado, a 2-8-2, was introduced and became the main freight engine from that time into the 50's. The Mikados were replaced by diesels in the 40's and 50's.

Dad told me about one job he worked on a Z. He said these 2-8-0 engines were rough riders. The day was hot and a heavy drag required maximum shoveling effort from the fireman. No coal stoker on most of those engines. He said that after a while the fireman was so hot and exhausted that he felt sorry for him and volunteered to take the shovel. Dad didn't say if the man stayed with the railroad or found another way to make a living, maybe in the freight house. And dad also never expressed a desire to become an engineer that I know of.

Class Z Consolidation

Communication between train crews was critical. Since my time on the railroad was before the introduction of radios all signals were given using various body appendages at one time or another either individually or in combination. Engine horn signals (whistles in the old days) were also in the mix. There were no brakeman signal training classes, or classes for anything else for that matter. The book of rules showed the basic positions but didn't capture the essence of good signaling. You basically learned all the signals by watching the other guys. If you didn't understand a signal don't do anything.

Miscommunication between train crews could result in serious breakage or injury. Most signals are given with a casual but clear motion. After a short time your signaling became more fluid and smooth and unintentionally quite cool and natural. When I go to an operating railroad museum or even a real railroad where hand signals are occasionally used instead of their radios it's interesting to note how the crews signal. They use all the right motions and do it just like in the pictures but they are a bit stilted and don't have the grace and smoothness of an experienced trainman.

Work train extra showing white flags. The engine is #1102. Roger Bass is on the right. Looks like so far they have managed to pick up one rock.

There were various degrees of intensity that are required in some situations in order to be clearly understood. The farther away the signaler was from the signalee the higher the intensity of the signal to be sure it was understood. A highball from the caboose of a long train would be an example of a very animated highball. Sometimes at night if you are on the back end of a very long train a lighted fuse swung over your head or thrown in the air is needed to let the engine crew know you are ready to go.

Fusees spit very hot sulpher and you needed to be careful where you swung them. Sometimes you had to raise the signaling effort to the highest level. If you're riding the point backing up to couple up to other cars, when you were about three car lengths away you swung your free arm up and down three times, then two car lengths, two swings, then one. If you're closing faster then usual you give the signal for three car lengths a little farther back and the engineer will slow down, but sometimes not enough. So you drop off of the stirrup before the cars couple up if you don't like to stop fast.

If it was apparent that the engineer is coming too fast you got more animated. You dropped off the car, extended your arms straight out from your sides and started wagging them alternately up and down. He would apply brake pressure accordingly. The more violent the wave the more brake pressure the engineer applied. In many cases there would be a very positive handshake of the couplers, a loud bang, and some dust shaken off both cars. You didn't want to be on the car when that happened. The correct coupling speed is no more than four miles an hour. Or so. Sometimes when

the engineer stopped a little short of coupling up, the brakeman raised his arm and a quick twist of the hand signaled the engineer to ease backward and couple up.

One of the more interesting moves was making a drop. Sometimes you wanted to spot a car on a dead end spur but the only way to get into it was engine first with the car behind the engine. You can get the car in but you can't get the engine out. So you needed to drop the car into the spur leaving the engine on the main line.

To do this one brakeman took his position at the spur switch. The other brakeman was on the stirrup of the car to be dropped. He backed up the engine and car far enough back from the switch to allow space for the move and gave the engineer a backward kick with one leg and the engineer knew it was going be a drop. The engineer accelerated forward rapidly. When the brakeman on the car felt he had sufficient speed he swung one arm from over his head in an arc that ended at the car's pin lifter. This was the signal for the engineer to make a slight brake reduction which gave the brakeman slack in the knuckles so he could pull the pin. When he got the slack and pulled the pin he kicked his leg out telling the engineer he's got the pin and the engineer rapidly accelerated, leaving a gap between the engine and the car. After the engine passed the switch the other brakeman threw the switch and the car rolled into the siding. Then the engine could back up and go in and spot the car. If the crew were wearing tutus you'd swear this little drama was a real life ballet. Sadly, there were no spectators around to appreciate this so you had to be satisfied with a move well done.

Sometimes the drop had to be done over again if the gap between the engine and car wasn't great enough to safely throw the switch, or if the brakeman at the switch felt the car wasn't going fast enough to get all the way into the spur he wouldn't open the switch. A car that stopped on a switch could be a real problem. The basic way to determine if a car was in the clear was to straddle the main track and extend your arm and see if you could touch the car on the switch. If you could the car was probably fouling the main. If it was marginal you would signal the engine to back very slowly until you were sure whether or not the car was in the clear. It seems that the length of a guy's arm had something to do with the success of this method. Cornering a car was the penalty, to say nothing about the bent grab irons on the engine.

If the brakeman at the switch didn't throw the switch the car ran into the slowing engine, coupled up, and you backed the engine further behind the switch and tried again. If the switch is thrown under the engine or under the car the curtain comes down and you are going to have a long intermission. Some of this stuff was easier to do then explain.

Then there's a variation called the Dutch drop. It's the same situation as the above except the track sloped down towards the spur and you relied on gravity to move the car independent of the engines. The brakeman applied the hand brakes on the car to be dropped and bled off the brake reservoir, releasing the air brakes. The engine had been uncoupled and sent down past the spur switch. When the engine was in the clear the man at the switch lined it up for the spur and the man on the car released the brakes and the car rolled down into the spur. The guy

81

on the car applied brakes as necessary to stop the car after it ran into the spur. On a good day you could actually spot the car at the correct door.

The West Allis switch run was a job that switched heavy industries along the North Western main line. I caught it once and that was enough. You didn't learn that job in a day. Or a week. Most of the plants had gated spurs that go into their factories. Engines cannot go into the buildings so if the crew had to pick up or set out a car deep inside the plant they had to keep a string of cars, usually flat cars, between the engine and the car being spotted or picked up. Some industries had their own little diesel engines or regular trucks with couplers that could move a few cars for internal switching. Allis Chalmers was one of the big industries in that territory, building tractors and other equipment. Another big company that comes to mind is the Harnischfeger Corporation. One of the not too uncommon occurrences in this district was to accidentally push cars through locked gates. The companies just hated that as did the railroad who had to pay for it.

Dad had a bit of a problem making a Dutch drop. A unionized industry, Press Steel Company, was on strike and they wanted to move a badly needed car into the plant. Train crews, also unionized, are not expected to cross picket lines. The railroads could easily handle situations like this. They sent officials out to the facility, one a qualified engineer, to do what the train crew wouldn't do. The total cast of characters in this scene include the railroad officials, the train crew, Press Steel officials and a number of police officers. At various times during union strikes or lockouts things of this type could become pretty volatile. The crew got off the engine and the management guys climbed on board.

The car had been uncoupled on the main line on the west side of National Avenue and the engine moved east over National Avenue and past the target spur. The car's air brakes held the car and it wouldn't move until its air reservoir had been bled. The brakeman hadn't set the hand brake. He bled off the reservoir and the car started rolling. He couldn't get to the hand brake on the front of the car and the car rolled towards the unguarded crossing. One of the officials saw the car coming, got on the car and set the hand brake but couldn't stop the car before it went over the crossing. He later testified that the box car just missed a car on National Avenue. The proper procedure would have been to first set the hand brake and then bleed off the reservoir, get on the car and release the brake when the crossing was protected. And the conductor should have seen the unfolding scenario and been on the crossing. There were a couple of mistakes there.

Rule 103 had been violated. The book of rules reads:

> *"When cars are pushed by an engine, except when shifting or making up trains in yards, a trainman must take a conspicuous position on the leading car and when switching over public crossings at grades not protected by a watchman or by gates, a member of the crew must protect the crossing, but will not place himself in such position on the crossing as to endanger his own safety. Conductors and yard engine foremen will be held responsible for seeing that movements such as described above are performed in a safe manner."*

Things were pretty cut and dried. The hearing transcription was eleven pages long and Dad got some time off to pursue other interests. He should have been guarding the crossing.

Rule G was another important rule that applied to all railroads. It had been a rule on individual roads for a long time and was finally made official by the government. It clearly prohibited employees from using alcohol while on duty or subject to call to duty. Now it probably applies to a number of other mind affecting agents as well. The rule was pretty strictly adhered to but I knew of one exception. I don't know where he came from or where he finally went but he was on a night job with us going to Milwaukee. He may have been a boomer on a student run because we had a flag-man on the back end along with him. When we stopped at a town to switch he simply went to the nearest saloon and got a shot and came back. Finally he was in such bad shape we put him in the caboose and told him to stay there.

The now defunct Fox Head Brewery was in Waukesha. They had a large cold water tank in the back of the building where we switched their cars. It was filled with shorties for use by the employees, responsibly, and they said they shared. None of us took a bottle but it was a nice gesture.

In earlier days there were rails called boomers. They were experienced guys that bounced from railroad to railroad, depending on who was hiring and how warm it was or how hungry they were. They never worked very long on one railroad and Rule G was often their downfall. One kind of boomer was pretty well accepted in many places, the telegrapher. They had a universal skill that could be used on all railroads but usually they didn't stay long enough with one railroad, for whatever reason, to get much seniority.

7

LIKE every other industry, there is a hierarchy on the railroad, formal or not. At the top are the operating people, starting with engineers, then trainmen and switchmen, at least in their own eyes. All of the supporting people doing the other necessary jobs to run a railroad no doubt think they are just as or even more important than the operating guys. And they are. How are you going to run a railroad if the section crews don't maintain the tracks or the signalmen don't keep the important green, yellow and red signal lights lit? The difference may be public exposure. Engineers whistling by in the cabs of their powerful locomotives, occasionally condescending to wave to the masses from their high perches, the crews on the stage on the back platform of their cabooses grandly waving to the people. Where's the romance of a lone signal maintainer trouble-shooting a trackside electrical cabinet or a track gang replacing a rail? What little kid ever said he wanted to be a signalman when he grew up? This could be the basis for a sociological study. And a lot of negative comments can be avoided if this volume is restricted to only non-railroad readers. Interestingly, everyone seemed to be pretty well satisfied with his situation. This was also true of my experience in the Navy. It was my experience that above a certain level in any organization ambitious people become very competitive and anything goes. Watch your back.

My next student run was on the east end way freight, train 670 from Monona yard to Milwaukee and 679 coming back. I had made that trip with Dad when I was in my teens.

He was the head brakeman so we rode on the engine. Our power was an old Mikado Class J steam engine, wheel arrangement 2-8-2. The J was the primary freight engine on the railroad at that time and for a few more years to come. The North Western had purchased 310 of these engines, built from 1913 to 1923. Recall that the Class Z production ended in 1913. By the time I rode this J they had been around a while. They were built to be hand fired and later were converted to stoker feeds. Most came with fairly short tenders but some had long tenders. Aesthetically the engines with long tenders looked better but function before form.

C. T. Felstead

Mikado #2490 posing in the classic rods down position in Monona Yard in Madison.
The small door at the lower front of the tender indicates that it had been converted to stoker feed.
This engine appears to have the long tender.

I climbed the vertical ladder and stepped into the cab. It was dark and drab and everything looked strange. I couldn't take it all in at once but there were a lot of different kinds of stuff everywhere. The front wall, called the back head, was pretty much covered with glass water gauges, valves, piping, white faced dials and I don't know what all. Across from me on the engineer's side of the cab were the long throttle and reversing levers and the whistle cord. The engineer also had a couple of air brake levers and some other stuff he needed at his left hand to operate the engine. Throw in a few unidentifiable objects and you have a rough idea of what the inside of a cab looked like. The lights in the cab apparently consisted of about two dim light bulbs enclosed in wire cages. The firebox butterfly doors were low dead center on the backhead. The back end of the cab was open to the tender. I think there was a grimy canvas roll at the top rear of the cab that could be dropped in bad weather. Or more likely there were canvas flaps on each side that could be closed.

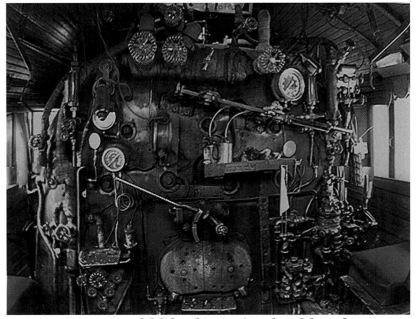

A restored Mikado engine backhead.
This is tidier than how a working
North Western J looked in the 40's.

There was a longitudinal bench on the fireman's side just barely wide enough to accommodate both the fireman and the brakeman. It was a pitiful affair, a broken down sagging cushion seat on a wooden bench with rags hanging out but it was serviceable. The fireman could check the fire by stepping down on a lever that swung the firebox doors open from the bottom, butterfly wing style. When the doors were opened the cab lit up with a bright warm orange glow that really improved the ambiance. By this time in its life, this engine had probably been retrofitted with a worm gear stoker feeding coal to the firebox from the tender relieving the fireman of most of his shoveling duties. The stoker was powered by a little steam turbine in the tender.

I looked out the side window, and way down and inside, tucked under the boiler, were the side rods and drivers. I was hanging out in space and momentarily had the definite feeling that this baby was going to roll over and crush me like a bug. I pulled my head in and looked across the cab toward the engineer's side and saw that he had the exact same problem. When you think about it, these two bad situations probably averaged out and this beast was probably going to stay upright, except when it went into a curve. Then we were going to live or die at the discretion of the engineer.

The tracks are four feet eight and one-half inches apart inside the balls of the rails. This engine was ten feet four inches wide over the cylinders, the widest part of the engine. The cab was about nine feet wide, or 16 inches narrower than the cylinders. Adjust for about five inches away from the inside of the rail to the outside face of the drivers and do the numbers. The side of the cab was hanging out about two feet outside the drivers. And don't forget the one foot or so my head was sticking out the window. Who wouldn't be a little bit concerned?

Two short blasts of the whistle and we got under way out the yard lead around a bend to the smash board guarding the Milwaukee Road main line tracks. A smash board is simply a pole across the track that protects the Milwaukee Road track. Dad got off the engine, opened the gate and we clickity-clacked over the diamond. We proceeded slowly, giving the hind brakeman time to close and lock the gate behind us and catch the caboose. We were headed out to Milwaukee on the way to Deerfield, then to

Cottage Grove. A few times engines ran through the smash board. When one engineer who did was asked if he was sleeping he admitted he was, "but not real sound."

Nobody explained anything to me so all that I picked up was the obvious. When we stopped at one town Dad said we were going to go up and ride in the dog house. I was good with that, whatever that was. We climbed down from the engine cab and walked to the back of the tender. There was a ladder that took us to the top of the tender. The rear end of the tender was a flat surface with a hatch for taking on water. The coal bunker with its slope sheet angled towards the engine was located in front of the water tank. The ratio between water and coal varied widely, depending on what kind of service the engine was designed for.

At the top of this tender there was a small box structure with windows on both sides and a door with a window, and a seat inside facing to the rear. The head brakemen had complained that there was not enough room for both the

fireman and brakeman on the bench in the cab so the railroad started building the dog houses on the tenders of the J's for the brakeman to ride in. The brakeman had to climb to the top of the tender, then climb back down to do any switching. If he had to open a switch ahead of the engine he had to walk the length of the tender and the engine.

As a practical matter the doghouse worked well on time freights but not on way freights. On time freight 594 there were only one or two stops between Madison and Chicago so the brakeman usually had a leisurely ride in the doghouse if the engine had one. On way freights there was too much getting on and off to make riding up there worthwhile.

The back of the cab roof had a lip on it to deflect the smoke up over the doghouse which was directly in line with the stack. Its effectiveness probably depended on how fast the train was going. The windows were so grimed up that they were almost opaque. Dad had the foresight to bring up a rag to wipe off the windows. From the brakeman's seat in the engine he could see down one side of the train. From the dog house located at the center of the tender he could see down both side of the train on curves.. He also had a great view of the passing scenery or the night sky if he had remembered to wipe off the windows. Since then I have seen just one picture of a J with a dog house. It was an interesting, pretty rare experience. Engineers were pretty intent on seeing where they were going and didn't check their side of the train much. A lot of people have been in the dog house but how many have ever ridden in one?

We arrived at Belton, where our track met the freight main line that goes from Chicago to the Twin Cities through Butler Yard. After calling the dispatcher and getting permission to go out on the main line, Dad opened the switches and we crossed over the westbound main and down the eastbound main towards what was then Madison yard. Dad headed us into the yard and we tied up.

R. M. Jorgenson Collection

Mikado 2455 with dog house. It has the original spoke wheel drivers.

C. T. Felstead

Mikado 2521 with dog house on the tender. The original spoke wheel drivers were replaced by the newer style boxpok wheels and the engine was designated J-A. Note the variation in tender styles.

It was a fairly small yard parallel to Mitchell Street in the heart of industrial Milwaukee. A couple things really caught your attention. One was the huge coke plant just across the street from the freight yard. I think it was the Solvey Coke plant. It was a long, very tall structure and at the top its full length was glowing in warm orange flames that lit up the whole area. The other attention-getter was invisible but all pervasive. There were open top gondolas full of raw cow hides that reeked to high heaven. Milwaukee was a big leather processor, probably because of the large number of unskilled eastern Europeans that came to Milwaukee that had that background or it was the only job they could get. Another entry level job. So this was our environment until tomorrow afternoon. The train crew slept in the caboose.

After a while you kind of got used to the smell. We broke out our bedrolls and packed it in. The next afternoon we headed back to Madison. That's about all I remember about that trip but it was a good memory.

Many years after it happened Dad told me a story about an experience he had on Mitchell Street during the depression. He was walking down the street during the day carrying his grip and bed roll on his way to the freight yard. He may have dead-headed over to Milwaukee on a passenger train and was walking to his caboose. He was stopped by one of Milwaukee's finest. The cop asked him who he was and what he was doing there. Dad told him he was a railroad man going from the depot to the rail yards. The cop made him open his grip, dump it out and unroll

Road bridge over the old C&NW roadbed, 2007.
Retro image of train 620, Madison to Milwaukee.
Head end power, R-1 or Class D Atlantic 4-4-2.
Later it was powered by an EMD E7 or E8.
Consist — mail car, baggage car, passenger car,
all heavyweights, circa early 1950's.
The same equipment was used both ways.

his bedroll on the sidewalk. Then he just looked at it and walked away. Even after all those years I could see the anger in Dad's face.

On one run I made on 670 and 679 between Madison and Milwaukee the conductor, Russell Sullivan, took great pride in his cooking as well as the appearance of his caboose. Across from the stove he had built a cupboard with a door that swung down to be used as a table. The cupboard had all the fixin's and pots and pans. We ate pretty well. At the end of the run the rear brakeman was expected to sweep out the caboose, platforms and steps. Yard crews were expected to replenish coal, drinking water, fusees and other supplies but that didn't always happen. Thankfully by this time the gondolas full of rotting cow hides were long gone.

Much later I had one embarrassing experience on 670. Late one night I got the call from the crew caller. We would get called an hour before we went on duty. It was one of those nights when you think you need just a little more time to wake up. Too much State Street? The phone rang a second time. Damn!

As I crossed the tracks at Johnson Street I looked down the yard tracks and saw the engine's headlight on dim, glowering in the dark. I didn't know engines could do that. I parked the car at the yard office and headed for the engine. It was very dark so I couldn't see if rose petals had been strewn in my path. I climbed up the steps onto the catwalk and up into the cab, dark except for the engineer's gauge lights. The engine crew was apparently very polite and understanding because nothing was said. At least not out loud.

The rear brakeman had put the engines on the train, did the brake test and lined the switches out of the yard for Milwaukee. The engineer pulled the whistle cord twice and opened the throttle. We headed out of the yard and around the curve towards the smash board. This time I, not Dad, opened the gate. I was pleased that I had something useful to do.

One night coming back on 679 we spotted a Black Angus steer standing sideways in the middle of the track but we couldn't stop. The cow looked at us and then disappeared under the nose of the engine. We heard a thud and the cow came flying up in the air angling ahead and to our right in the exact position he was in when we first saw him. He looked perfectly fine, then disappeared out of our headlight into the night. The knuckle no doubt caught him just under his center of gravity and this cow jumped over the moon. The railroad is responsible for fence lines along its rails so the farmer no doubt put a claim against the company. The face of the knuckle had a layer of Black Angus hair on it.

North Western cabooses were spartan affairs, nothing fancy but serviceable. The earliest cabooses were basically box cars with windows and doors. A North Western conductor is credited with the idea for the cupola. He was in a boxcar with a hole in the roof, got some boxes, climbed up and looked out the top. It was apparently a grand view and the cupola was born. He no doubt got the Employee of the Month Award.

The North Western settled on a more or less standard design in the 1890's and stuck with that footprint through the life of these cabooses. The early cabooses had wood underframes which didn't hold up too well as trains got longer and faster. The coupler slack action could subject the caboose and its crew to some pretty violent starts and stops. The railroad replaced the wood with steel underframes, usually a main beam down the middle and a steel sill on each side. Newer cabooses were built with a steel underframe.

Many cabooses went through several modifications but no radical changes from the original design. Cabooses were thirty feet long. Counting the three foot platforms on each end, they were about thirty-six feet long. The number of windows evolved through the years. The two windows on each end were eliminated to reduce injuries in the event of an accident but a window in each door was kept. The final configuration was three windows on one side and five on the other.

Cabooses were referred to as way cars by the North Western and eastern railroads but trainmen called them cabooses as did the western railroads. There is a long list of other slang names that were used, not all complimentary, by railroaders all over the country. The North Western cabooses were among the longest on any railroad. Up until the late 50's each regular conductor had an assigned caboose. Some men took great pride in them, curtains on the windows, rugs on the floor, cabinets for storing food and pans.

Almost from the beginning cabooses were equipped primarily with old passenger car four-wheel trucks, wheels five feet on center and the main supports on these trucks were wood

Wood caboose passenger trucks.
The horizontal member and cross beams
on each end were wood. The springs
were both coil and leaf springs.

beams. These old trucks and wooden cabooses that would flex probably gave the best ride of any caboose in the country. The wood-beamed trucks lasted well into the sixties.

The cupola was not a real safe place to ride. Unlike passenger cars, freight cars have significant travel in their couplers. And the slack runs in and out. On a long train when the engineer starts out he moves very slowly, taking the slack out of each car and in the caboose you can hear the slack running out. The engine can move pretty far on a long train and the caboose still hasn't moved when the slack is in. The guys in the caboose like to hear a nice even rhythm as the slack is taken up. If you hear a rapid series of bangs getting closer and louder you really want to hang on. The caboose can literally jump ahead. Same deal when you are coming to a stop. The slack runs in with about the same sound and you stop pretty quick. The guys on the engine know when the engineer made a fast stop with the slack out because as the slack runs in, they can feel the train shoving the engine forward. And they wonder what the guys in the caboose are discussing, possibly something about ancestry. It could get ugly back there.

The slack can be useful on very heavy trains. Starting a train with the slack out, you are starting out pulling the total weight of the train from a dead stop. The engines won't always do that. The engineer will back up, getting slack on the head end cars and then move forward. Now he is starting the front part of his train one car at a time. Once the engine gets moving it can pull the rest of the train that still has the slack out. Late model steam engines often had steam powered boosters to give the main drivers a hand starting the train. The booster was usually the lead truck on the tender.

The engineers and firemen I worked with were almost all pretty good men, capable and conscientious and they kept the train on the tracks. There are always some exceptions. For instance, recall that the Dakota 400 sideswiped a switch engine in Monona Yard and put the lead unit on the ground. I suspect the switch engine met the same fate.

I caught a couple trips with one fireman who must have had a day job. As soon as we started out he would settle back and go to sleep. And he slept very well. The good news is that it didn't affect the operation of the train. My job was to keep an eye on the left side of the train. His job was to look out the front window. However, when he rested he slumped down which gave me a good 180 degree view out of the left side of the engine. Many years later I was relieved to learn that he never did become an engineer.

Some trainmen were aware of the characteristics of their engineer. Some were really good train handlers, others were known as fast engineers. If you're on a job that you've made your basic day based on miles, a fast engineer will get you home sooner for the same amount of pay.

There are a lot of things to consider in train handling. Even though it doesn't look like it, there are small uphill and downhill grades on railroad tracks. And as mentioned, the slack also runs in and out on the road. Engineers have to know the road, their train and how to use the throttle, train brakes and engine brakes, either independently or in combination to minimize slack action. They were all pretty good at train handling.

In the late twenties many cabooses went through the Chicago shops and cupolas, which were no longer effective, were removed. In the 30's some cabooses were converted from cupola to bay window. Some of these cabooses were equipped with new steel trucks which were no doubt easier to maintain. They did not ride as well as the old passenger car wood beamed trucks but required less maintenance. The wood beam cabooses were still primarily used on over the road trains because they gave the best ride. On a few occasions, just for the novelty of it, I would ride in the cupola and the seldom used seats were always dusty.

In the 50's there were at least three variations of the standard caboose. The original with cupola, the original with no cupola and cabooses with no cupolas but bay windows added. The bay windows were introduced in about 1937. The interiors of these cabooses were redesigned to accommodate a passenger type seat on each side. The seat backs could be swung back and forth over the seat depending on the direction the train was going so the crew could always look ahead. The bay window cabooses prevented a lot of cinders flying in the crew's eyes.

On the next pages are photos of the interior of caboose 11546 which was built in 1915. The inside was unchanged from when it was built except for the removal of the cupola. Note that the conductor's desk chair is missing.

The interiors of the wooden cupola cabooses had long benches on each side with lids that opened up. On these benches were cushions filled with horse hair. On one side of the caboose the bench ran from the end wall to the stove. There was a short bench from the stove to the wall under the cupola. That side had three windows. On the other side the bench ran from the end of the caboose to the conductor's desk. There were five windows on that side.

In the cupola area under the upper level seats there were storage bins for various and sundries and coal for the stove. Beyond the cupola to the end was the wash basin on one side and a clothes closet and the rest room on the other. On a well-equipped caboose the rest room actually had a seat. Let's leave it at that. The sink in the caboose pictured is probably the one that was installed in 1915 and has obviously held up very well. They don't build 'em like that anymore.

This was the age when trainmen were very conscious of recycling, reducing energy, and saving the planet. The emissions from the caboose went directly back to nature via the railroad track. This was also true of passenger trains, and walking down the tracks one would be prudent to watch one's step. Nowadays that stuff goes through an expensive, energy recycling process for the sake of protecting the environment. Saving the planet costs money. That's progress. And the little sign in the little room that said **PLEASE DO NOT FLUSH WHEN TRAIN IS STANDING IN THE STATION** became a quant artifact.

Interior of caboose 11546

North Western cabooses usually did not have a tool box under the belly, like many other railroads did. Necessary equipment for cabooses were spare knuckles, coupler pins and air hoses. Also required was a wrench to replace leaking air hoses. These supplies and whatever else was necessary were stored in the benches in the caboose. The 11546 came with a knuckle in one of the benches. Torpedoes, fusees and a red flag were usually readily available at one end of the caboose or the other. When trainmen slept in cabooses on regular jobs they often brought bed springs and a pad for maximum comfort. One side of the spring was attached to wall brackets and the aisle side was held up by a leg on each corner.

By the late 50's the railroad made arrangements with motels for their crews and yard transportation or cabs were provided to pick up and deliver them. Train crews no longer slept in cabooses.

The new steel cabooses were introduced in the late 50's and were equipped with generators and electric lights. They were still very spartan, no frills. Some other railroads' cabooses in comparison looked like nicely fitted out private cars.

Eventually the railroad went to pooled cabooses. Switchmen picked the next available caboose off the caboose track and coupled it onto the back of your train. You needed to check the supplies on board before you left town.

John C. La Rue Jr. Collection

Standard caboose, early 1900's design

Trainmen were very time conscious. Pocket watches were required into the 50's and maybe beyond but with the advent of battery powered watches, wrist watches became more common. I didn't have a railroad watch but would borrow dad's if he was off duty or in freight service and I was working passenger trains. Trains could arrive ahead of schedule but could not leave before their scheduled time of departure without the dispatcher's permission.

John C. La Rue Jr. Collection

Some caboose cupolas were removed when cabooses were shopped in the late 20's. Cabooses with wood beams were fitted with a steel center beam and a sill beam on each side.

John C. La Rue Jr. Collection

Final configuration of many wood cabooses in the second half of the 30's

Trainmen were also very conscious of days, months, etc. This was manifested by the calendars often found hanging on caboose walls. These calendars were also found in mechanics' work places and other primarily male-dominated domains. Often careful scrutiny of these calendars might show that the month, much less the year, may not be the correct one displayed under the picture. By today's standards these calendars could probably be considered more artful than prurient. They were pretty tame. Occasionally a wife or some other woman would visit a caboose. Other than the usual mandatory female ***oh my goodness!*** they wouldn't really be shocked.

John C. La Rue Jr. Collection

Bay window old-timer in company work train service, 1969

Cabooses were also equipped to provide hot, er, warm water. But that depended on whether or not the stove was lit. Behind and above the stove there was a metal water tank equipped with a faucet attached to the wall. This water was not drinkable but was O.K. for washing dishes and morning ablutions.

The new steel cabooses came in a different color. An official named Zito decided that the traditional red caboose color was not as visible as a pale yellow. About that time fire engines were painted a light yellow to supposedly make them more visible. Red appears black at night. Fire fighters were not particularly crazy about the new color and the yellow color of their pumpers was often changed back to the traditional red. The new cabooses as well as new or repainted engines were painted with the new yellow. Mr. Zito may have won the Employee of the Month Award for that perceived improvement.

The color was pretty bad, it made the equipment look anemic and did not weather well. It faded and the equipment looked progressively worse. Finally the railroad went back to the traditional North Western yellow color and Mr. Zito may have lost his executive parking space. An aging Zito yellow caboose appears elsewhere in these pages.

The new steel cabooses were built with a number of windows but because of incidents with stone throwers all the windows were blanked out except the ones in the bay window area. On rare occasions people shot at trains. Dad had an unfortunate experience one night going through Evansville. Someone threw a rock through an open window and hit him on the head. He was taken to the hospital and checked out O.K.

I had worked on the railroad for about two years before somebody noticed I had swung onto the back end of a moving car which was coupled to a following car. My partner pointed out that if you misjudged the stirrup or the ladder rung you were grabbing for you'd probably fall between the cars with predictable results. That

Original steel caboose, late 50's

Steel caboose with windows blanked out

sticks in your mind. If you try to get on the front end of a moving car and can't hang on, hopefully you will bounce off the car. That made a lot of sense. There were two kinds of cars that you don't want to get on when they are moving, flat cars and tank cars. They have stirrups but nothing to hang onto above the floor level.

We used to get on and off moving cars when we thought we could do it safely. Some people had a higher tolerance for risk than others and I guess I was one of them.

One day I caught the Beloit switch run. Actually Beloit had three switch jobs, two working out of Monona Yard and one that switched and tied up in Beloit. Tommy Jacobson worked the Beloit job for quite a few years. He was running M-2 and M-3 steamers and there was an engine watchman and another man that coaled up his engine every night. Once a month the engine went to Monona Yard for servicing. Diesels finally replaced the old-timers.

We had come out of Beloit and stopped at Evansville. We were running with two Geeps. The conductor and rear brakeman were at the depot and the engines, for some reason, were about ten car lengths east of the depot. I was between the engines and the Evansville depot. I signaled the engineer to come forward toward the depot. I was four or five car lengths away from the depot and ahead of the engines and as they approached I thought they were coming pretty fast but I went for it. I remember going for the hand rails and step and the next thing I was aware of was that I was lying flat on my back in the dirt just beyond the track ballast looking up at the underside of the moving engine which was rapidly coming to a stop.

That bouncing off theory really worked. I felt fine, very relieved, and got up and brushed myself off. Everything still seemed to be working. I had no abrasions, aches or pains and surprising, no aftereffects. I walked up to the cab and I could see the white face of the engineer. Actually he always looked pretty pale. He said he thought that I was going to walk up to the depot so he didn't slow down. Then he slowly moved ahead and I swung onto the footboard at the back of the trailing engine. I recently found out at one of the retiree's breakfasts that that engineer had a pretty universal reputation of being hard on his firemen and brakemen. Today, trainmen are not permitted to get on or off moving equipment. In some cases with only an engineer and conductor on the train, the conductor is required to assist the engineer on and off the train if needed.

Besides doubling a hill there are a number of other types of train handling situations that are fairly common. When a freight train reaches its destination yard there are times when there is no clear yard track long enough to hold the train. In that case you simply double into the yard, leaving part of your train on one track and the rest on another clear track. Or you park your train on the main line and let the switch crew deal with it. If it takes longer than fifteen minutes to yard your train after you hit the yard limit board extra money is earned. This encourages switchmen and yardmasters to have space available when your train arrives.

Years ago the North Western's Madison Division was mostly double-tracked. With the advent of the I-System making trucks more efficient and autos able to get people places faster, the railroads went into decline, both freight and passenger service. I remember taking train loads of Portland cement cars to South Beloit for the building of I-90 and thinking that we were hanging ourselves with our own rope. As fewer trains ran because of the new highways the need for two main line track was reduced to the point where it became more cost-effective to pick up one main and use the remaining one for trains running in both directions. Parts of the old mains were left in place to be used for long passing tracks.

Dwight Eisenhower was the father of the Interstate System. In 1919 he participated in a cross-country military convoy to the west coast and it was not a good trip. As a result he realized the value of a good road system. His experience with good roads in Europe during WW II further reinforced that belief. Thanks to the general we now have a modern national highway network which complements our rail system.

Passenger trains were superior to freight trains even though the freights made the money and passenger trains operated at a loss. Passenger trains for show, freights for dough. With both types using the same track conflicts were bound to occur. Normally a freight train would take the siding and wait for the passenger train to go by. There were strict requirements as to when a freight had to be in the clear for a passenger train or at what point they were supposed to meet and they were clearly spelled out in train orders from the dispatcher. Also, the time table showed the arrival times of passenger trains at all points and freights had to clear the main at least fifteen minutes before the scheduled arrival of the passenger train.

At times, freight trains were too long to fit in a siding. Thus the saw-by. Since passenger trains were superior and therefore almost always held the main, the freight had to make the passing as painless as possible for the passenger train. To do this, the freight headed into the too short passing track and pulled down to the other end. The back of the freight would still be on the main. The engineer left his head-light on bright to indicate to the approaching passenger train that the freight was not in the clear. Both trains had been informed of this meet by the dispatcher. There is one kind of meet that should be avoided. It's called a cornfield meet, where two trains are going different directions toward the same point on the same track. In the old days they used

to do that intentionally for entertainment, occasionally killing spectators.

The passenger train pulled down the main past the freight on the siding to the other end and stopped. As soon as the passenger train cleared the switch ahead of the freight engine the freight's head brakeman opened that switch and it pulled out onto the main behind the passenger train. As the caboose cleared the main on the back end of the siding the rear brakeman lined the switch for the main line and the passenger train went on about its business. Sometimes a thoughtful head brakeman on the passenger train or God forbid, the fireman, would walk up and close the switch after the caboose cleared the main. Firemen were basically non-revenue passengers on diesels but you didn't read that here. I'm going to get letters. As the caboose moved out on the main at the other end of the passing track the rear brakeman closed that switch and everything was back to normal. If the passenger train is there first it pulls down to the other end of the siding and hopefully the head brakeman on the passenger train will open the switch into the siding for the freight.

When a freight train fits in the siding and in the clear and the switch is lined for the main, the engine headlight is dimmed telling the oncoming engineer that he has a clear track. In the situation when one train, usually a freight, is overtaken by another, usually a passenger train, if the freight is on the main the marker lights on the caboose both show red. There will also be some red fusees burning and sometimes two torpedoes set to clearly make the point that there is somebody ahead. A torpedo is a small explosive device that is clamped on the ball of the rail on the engineer's side that makes a very loud bang when the engine's wheels roll over it. Two torpedoes, set about twenty feet or more apart, are used to make sure the engineer gets the message that there could be something ahead. If the freight is in a siding and in the clear one caboose marker light shows green, the other red, indicating to the oncoming engineer that he has a clear track. Rather than going to the trouble of rotating the marker light in it's bracket we usually took if down and set it on the caboose platform with a green light showing.

Steam power on the North Western wasn't phased out until 1956 so most of the engine crews I worked with had experience firing steam engines. Engineers were probably partly the result of a self-selection process. Long hours shoveling coal into the red hot maws of the fire-boxes took its physical toll. Engine cabs were poorly ventilated, a plus in winter but miserable in the summer heat. Firemen that could handle those difficult conditions were more likely to stay and go on to become engineers.

To become an engineer there was another bar to clear. These men had to study and learn the theory and practice of the steam engine and later, diesel-electrics, and were required to take federal examinations to qualify for their licenses. Often they had to pay for their own training. After that they patiently bided their time in the long line of seniority succession to finally take their place in the right-hand seat of those fire-breathing monsters and later the more genteel diesels. By the mid-1950's all of these men were diesel engine drivers.

Briefly there was one major difference between freight and passenger steam engines and that was the size of the drivers. The wheel configuration for all steamers was pilot, drivers, and trailing trucks though the one constant was they all had drivers. A Pacific 4-6-2, oo-OOO-o, had four pilot wheels or pony trucks, six driving wheels and two trailing wheels. In general terms the pony trucks guided the engine down the tracks and led it into curves. Fast passenger engines always had four pony wheels. The drivers were the powered wheels and carried most of the engine's weight. The trailers supported the fire box.

C&NW Class E-2 Pacific. These engines pulled the first 400's which went into service in1937 pulling old, refurbished heavy-weight cars. These trains were replaced by streamlined trains in 1939, powered by a pair of EMD E3's. The twelve E-2's as well as almost all of the rest of the North Western steamers were gone by the end of 1956.

Engines could be divided into four parts front to back. First was the smoke box and the cylinders below, then the longest part, the boiler, third the fire box and finally the crew cab. Directly behind the cab was the tender which carried the coal and water. Some engines were oil fired. The first two engines fitted out for the 400's when they went into service in 1935 were oil fired and required fewer stops than if they had been coal fired. Most latter-day engines had coal stokers to feed the firebox which made the fireman's job a lot easier. At some point, as engines got bigger a fireman could not shovel coal fast enough to keep up the steam pressure. Sometimes a second fireman was added on the non-stoker fed engines but that was only a stop-gap measure. The Class D's, which weren't stoker equipped, sometimes had to run with two firemen to keep the steam up when they were pulling heavy troop trains during WWII.

In its simplest terms, the fire in the firebox heated the water in the boiler. The boiler, which was full of water, had a multitude of pipes called flues running through it which ran from the firebox forward to the smoke box. The heat and smoke traveled from the firebox through the flues to the smoke box, heating the water in the boiler into steam. The steam was piped into the cylinders in front of the drivers.

The main drive rods were connected to the cylinder pistons and to the offset main crank pin on one driver, usually the second one, on each side of the engine. From the main crank pin, side rods were connected to offset crank pins on the other drivers. The weight of these offset crank pins and rods were counter weighted on the opposite side of the wheels to keep the wheels in balance. When the engineer opened the throttle it let steam into the cylinders, alternately forcing the pistons in and out which pushed the drive rods and the wheels started to turn.

Some engine drivers were balanced to run at speeds up to 90 miles per hour. These drivers were finely balanced for high speeds with lead weights much like car wheels today. A few

Side rods and counterweight detail on an H-1.

freight Mikados were balanced to run at 70 m.p.h., probably for use in passenger service. Freight train speed limit was 55 m.p.h.

The exhaust steam from the cylinders went up into the smoke box forcing smoke from the firebox up and out the stack. Some of the exhaust steam went back to fan the fire in the firebox. All this to get your rhythmic chug, chug, chug and corresponding puff, puff, puff. When the engine is not moving it has air compressors to stoke the fires, which makes it sound like the engine is breathing. Some may feel that this

description of how a steam engine works is a bit simplistic. They're right. A diagram showing the nomenclature of a steam engine names over three hundred parts. Actually there are thousands. Maybe this will spur some readers on to do some research on these wonderful old machines that tied our vast nation together. Just to emphasize the point, at one time you were never more than twelve miles from a railroad track in the state of Iowa. Another source said that distance was only seven miles. In any case a farmer and his team could usually get his product to town and get back to the farm on the same day. The longest section of straight track in the nation is 73 miles long, located in Michigan.

One of the results of the engine crew not watching the water gauges was that if an engine under steam ran out of water it blew up, killing anyone on and around the engine. Pieces of the engine were sometimes found as far as a mile away after an explosion. The secret is to never let the water level get below the top of the crown sheet. The crown sheet is the top of the fire box and when an engine runs out of water the crown sheet drops into the fire box As a result of the steam pressure, the boiler may be completely blown away leaving only the engine frame and the wheels.

There was an inverse relationship between speed and power. Bigger wheels, more speed and less power, smaller wheels more power, less speed for the same cylinder size and steam pressure. The drivers on some passenger engines were over seven feet high. Steam engines could go the same speed forward or backward. At some speed steam engines started to hop. This was because the driving rods connected to the drivers are off-set from the center of the axle and the corresponding counter weights on each wheel weren't in exact balance. This imbalance also caused pounding on the rails, doing damage over time. The engineer knew he was getting close to the edge when the engine started to hop. If they manage to stay on the rails, at some speed steam engines will self-destruct, throwing themselves apart.

There were usually two domes on the top of the boiler. The one in front is the sand dome. The second one closer to the cab is the steam dome. The sand domes held fine sand that could be delivered by pipes leading to the front and back of the driving wheels by the engineer as needed to provide traction and control wheel slippage. The steam dome held the linkage that connected to the engineer's throttle controlling the steam pressure that went to the cylinders, thus controlling the engine speed. It also held the reversing mechanism.

The reversing lever located in the cab was called the Johnson Bar. On some engines this bar was difficult for the engineer to move and was sometimes power assisted. A black roundhouse guy named Johnson invented the power assist. At the back of the boiler just ahead of the cab there was a small steam powered electrical generator that provided the power for the engine's lights. The engine steam whistle was usually also located in that area.

In the early 1950's a recording was made of steam engines going up the grade through the Baraboo Hills. The engines were Class E Pacifics, 4-6-2 passenger engines, and Class J Mikados, 2-8-2 freight engines. Japan had placed the first order for the 2-8-2 wheel arrangement, thus the name. The sounds of their whistles echoing through the hills was haunting. One track in particular was especially dramatic. It was a Mikado pulling its heart out trying to make it up the grade. The engine went along at a very slow, steady chug, chug, chug, then a rapid chugchugchugchugchug as the drivers slipped, spinning, then the sound quickly

dropped back to the slow rhythm as the engineer backed off on the throttle. Then another rapid sequence. It was in the fall, raining, and wet leaves probably covered the tracks. Sanding the rails helped but didn't completely solve his problem. With a lot of patience and skill he probably made it to the top of the hill without doubling.

In 1959, time freight 471 that ran from Proviso Yard in Chicago to the Twin Cities was routed from the Adams line to the Madison line. The Madison District handled it from Janesville to Elroy. It was powered by three F units, 3's or 7's painted in freight colors, green, yellow, and black. They were very handsome engines. A Wisconsin Division crew brought the train into the Janesville yard and the Madison crew was waiting at the yard office. It would move slowly into the yard and before it got to us the incoming crew would climb off the engine. The train did not stop. The engine crew and I threw our stuff up into the cab and climbed aboard. You really needed to be there when she came in because it did not wait. Then we'd drag along slowly because the crew change was done the same way for the hind end crew, conductor and rear brakeman. No stopping. It was a long train and the engineer had to guess when they should have been aboard because there were no radios in those days. Then he'd open the throttle and we'd head for Madison.

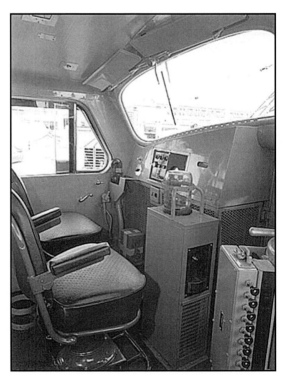

F unit cab. Fireman on the left, brakeman in the middle and engineer on the right

Train 471 and its opposite, 472, were true time freights and used to be known as maintrackers. They didn't go into yards and when they stopped to change crews they held the main. If they were dropping off or picking up cars, the engines were cut off and the yard switch engine came out on the main and did the switching. These two jobs may have been the purest form of maintracker since they didn't even stop to change crews.

There was no stopping to set out or pick up cars except at Monona Yard. There, by union rules, the switch crew did any switching that was needed. We'd stop at the west end of the yard just before the Commercial Avenue crossing which was protected by flashing lights.

The main line at Monona Yard between road crossings was about a mile long and it could probably hold about a

Ghost of time freight 471 out of Janesville for Elroy behind F7's

hundred cars. Those time freights were long trains and may have occasionally blocked one of the crossings. Going westbound the back end of the train could block Johnson Street, a fairly busy street so we made these movements as quickly as possible. Trains could legally block streets for a certain number of minutes. After that the conductor could get a ticket from the local police.

The switch engine was always waiting on the other main. They had a short block of cars for our train and would take off some Madison cars blocked on the front of our train. I got on the ground and cut off the engines and sent them down the track past a set of cross-over switches. When our engines were clear of the switches the switch crew backed in and pulled off the Madison cars, put them on the other main and backed in and coupled up the new cars for our train. Even though the crossing lights were flashing I guarded the crossing for these movements using fusees, waving cars through when the crossing was clear.

One night when Commercial Avenue was blocked by the switch engine going back and forth there was one car waiting to get through. The guy was pretty impatient and before the freight cars cleared the crossing he didn't wait for the crossing to clear. He came around the end of the box car towards me moving pretty fast. I stepped back and as he came by I threw the fusee at his windshield. I don't know how he felt about that but I felt a whole lot better. And golly, I certainly hope that the hellfire sulfur from the fusee didn't damage his paint job!

I thought he might want to come back and discuss the incident but when the crossing was cleared again nobody was there. When the switch engine was clear I backed up the engines, coupled up and we headed out for Elroy. The crew change was done the same way at Elroy. The train didn't stop.

That train, one each way, was the only time freight through Madison. All the rest of our movements were way freights, extras, or work trains. And, of course, passenger trains. Trains 471 and 472 ran through Madison to relieve congestion on the Adams line. The time freight did this for two or three years, 1959-61. Sometime later in the sixties Dad told me that the curved track west of the Elroy depot had a novel speed limit of sorts. Trains could not run at speeds roughly between 12 and 17 miles an hour or cars could derail. Because of the track condition the cars went into a rocking motion and could go off the track.

Coming eastbound from St. Paul it was train number 472. The crew change drill was the same at Elroy and Janesville, no stopping. I don't remember if we stopped in Madison for cars when we went eastbound.

Ghost of time freight 472 out of Elroy for Janesville behind F3's

116

One of the engineers had a coffee pot he brought along on this job and made coffee. He'd connect it to something in one of the electrical cabinets and make coffee. I never did figure out how he got a voltage match. I think these engines had 80 volt circuits so maybe if you waited long enough a 110 volt coffee maker would make you some coffee. It seemed to take quite a while. One night he plugged it in and after an appropriate interval went to pour himself a cup. It hadn't brewed. He opened the door on the fireman's side and very angrily flung it out and went back and took his seat. He must have spotted it on the next east bound trip, which was in daylight, because on our next night run going west he stopped the train, got off and retrieved the coffee pot and we went on our way. There was no conversation during these little episodes.

One trip going west it was late at night, probably about bar closing time. A car was coming down the road from the left. We whistled the crossing and the car did not slow down. Whatever his intentions were, at the last minute he apparently decided he wasn't going to beat the train. He hit the brakes, swerved left into the other lane, swerved back into his, and then left again, straight down what was probably about a fifteen foot embankment. If he'd just kept going he would probably have made it. It's called bet your life. We didn't know how things worked out for him but wished him the best.

I had an interesting experience one night on that same stretch of track. The track was a very long curve with a highway running parallel to it on the outside of the curve. A couple miles ahead we saw a single headlight. Nothing real unusual but it catches your eye since cars usually have two lights. As it came closer it seemed to be moving along at a leisurely pace, maybe about the speed of a freight train. A car with one light out? It wasn't a motorcycle because there was no tell-tale jiggle of the light. Nobody said anything but we all noticed it. And the light came steadily closer. On F units the brakeman's seat is in the middle of the cab between the engineer's control stand and the fireman's seat. The engine crew turned in their seats ready to stand up. The fireman stood up and I was now standing behind my seat. No words, action said it all. I knew what I was going to do. If it was what it could have been I was going out the engineer's side which was on the inside of the curve. If anything happened, some physical law or other told me that stuff would tend to move out and away from the inside of a curve. We could finally see the separation between the road and the track. It was a slow moving car with one light out.

Dad often ran this job. He'd had an operation on his ears and had a lot of trouble with his balance. He'd been off for a while and finally had to go back to work. This was a good job for him because, for the conductor and rear brakeman, it was just riding. Dad told me his balance was so bad that he couldn't get off the moving train without going down. He'd throw his bag off and then get off and fall down. He said he got off on the opposite side of the caboose from his brakeman and yard office so nobody would know what was happening. I would guess that he got off the front end of the caboose so by the time the slow moving caboose went by he was back on his feet. The same thing at Elroy. I felt so helpless and have not gotten that mental picture out of my mind to this day.

8

ONE evening I was riding the head end of 594, the time freight heading for Proviso Yard in Chicago. The head end cars were refrigerator cars with meat from Oscar Mayer as usual. As we approached the Madison depot I recalled the night I was on the platform as a baggage handler six or seven years ago when the three EMD GP7 demonstrators instead of the old J steam engine came in and stopped at the Blair Street crossing. Who'd a thought? At Proviso Yard, Yard Nine, the

receiving yard, I cut off the engines and sent them down the engine house lead and headed back to try and find the caboose. It is a very big yard and it was dark. When you found it you got aboard, spread your bed roll out on a bunk and tried to get some sleep.

A yard that big is a great place to listen to a railroad symphony and it is a beautiful sound. The program is the switch list. The bass drum bang of a string of cars coupling up a bit too hard, the piccolo sound of the wheel flanges squealing on the curves of the rails as they go through switches. A beginning clarinet player can easily replicate the sound of the steel-flanged squeal. The mellow trombone sounds of the diesel switchers revving up and idling back and the triangle chime of coupler pin linkages jingling. The steady rhythmic beat of a kettle drum as a string of cars rolls over the track joints. Occasionally there are two loud blasts of an air horn as part of the symphony rolls out of town. There are no intermissions.

The symphony put you to sleep. For a while. Then you're awakened by a gradually increasing brightness in the caboose. You hear the low rumble of the diesel switcher's engine getting louder and louder. The light becomes painfully bright and you know what's coming. Then clunk-lurch. We are coupled up. The diesel's headlight seems to be directly in line with the window in the door of the caboose. The guy who established the height of the caboose end windows and the guy who decided where the engine headlight should go were obviously in collusion or maybe it was the same guy. A compassionate engineer may dim the headlight but don't bet on it. A few moments of caboose-filling brilliant light, the sound of the idling diesel, and then the crunch of footsteps on cinders as the switchman walked to the other end of our caboose to pull the pin, uncoupling us from our train. The switchman gave the engineer the backup signal and swung up on the bottom step of the caboose platform. You knew there was slack in the couplers from the impact so you waited for the jerk as the engine backed up. We are now groggy passengers bound for the caboose track and a string of other cabooses, some occupied. After some back and forth'n through the yard we were buckled on to the rest of the way cars on the caboose track. Again the crunch of boots on gravel as the switchman walked back to the engine. Then the metallic clink as he pulled the pin on the caboose's coupler. The engineer notched up the throttle and the light and sounds faded away. Now it's time to get some undisturbed sleep. And listen to the sounds of the symphony.

One night in Proviso Yard I sent the engines to the ramp and started walking back through the yard to the caboose. I managed to find the right track and walked down the alley between the box cars. In a big yard sometimes it was hard to find your caboose. One of the key things was to know its number. You really don't want to go around knocking on caboose doors. Some crews marked their cabooses with unique stuff that clearly identified them. Sometimes it was a broom nailed to the cupola. Others guys nailed items like a shiny pie tin or an old hub cap on the ends of their cabooses.

The moon was full, very bright and directly overhead. I turned off my lantern and it was almost like daylight. I was walking along, enjoying the moonlight in the valley between boxcars when I heard the solid thud of boots hitting the cinders about ten feet behind me. I turned around and found myself looking into a bright light. The voice behind the light said *"Don't move!"* And I knew it had to be a railroad cop. He politely inquired as to what I might be doing in his yard and I told him I was a brakeman going back to my caboose. I knew that he could tell by my outfit that I was a brakeman. He told me to never walk through the yards at night without showing a light because there were some bad guys out here that shouldn't be, they were up to no good, and they didn't show lights. The railroad police carry heat. We chatted awhile and he told me some stories about what goes on in the yards after dark. He said sometimes gangs break into boxcars and steal the entire contents. At one point North Western employees were involved. Break-ins and theft were a continuing problem then and probably still are today. So let your little light shine. The railroad detectives or police were well-trained, often with the local police departments.

Proviso Yard was a good place for people who liked to travel by train but weren't interested in paying. There were trains going to all points north and west. During the depression years masses of regular people, men, women and kids, rode the rails to try to survive. Many were killed or injured. Others were hobos, tramps, and bums. In the first half of the twentieth century railroad police were often feared. There were so many riders that sometimes the cops got pretty tough with people riding the freights.

In those days these railroad policemen were often referred to as railroad bulls. In the 40's when the economy got better ordinary people stopped riding the trains.

Hobos would work for their meals, bums wouldn't. Many of these vagabonds followed a more or less regular routine, heading south for the winter, north for the summer, sometimes looking for seasonal jobs depending on their net worth. Today there are occasional upstanding citizens that ride the freights purely for excitement and the feeling of freedom.

After getting up in the morning there was nothing to do until the return trip on 591 that afternoon. I went over to town, Bellwood, and wandered around. It was a pretty safe town during the day but at night it could get a little dicey. I don't remember much about what I did there. Probably visited a library, museum or some other cultural points of interest.

One summer evening in late 1956 or '57 I was the head brakeman on 594, the time freight from Monona Yard to Proviso Yard 9. The sun had set and it was now deep twilight. I looked to the south and saw an unforgettable sight. We were running parallel to a seemingly endless row of old steam engines on the dead line about a half-mile away, sitting cold and lifeless, knuckle to knuckle. They were of all

Steam engine dead line in Proviso Yard

122

sizes, black silhouettes seemingly part of the landscape. It could have been a row of old elephants, tail to trunk. For me it was a moment in time, never to be forgotten or seen again. If I'd had the time and a camera I would have taken a final portrait of some of those ugly old brutes that had their own grace and power. They would be stripped of any parts that may have had some further value and sold to scrap dealers for so many pennies per pound, like a herd of steers at the slaughter house.

The North Western, unlike some other large railroads, almost never sold or donated any of their old steamers to towns or museums. However, there are three R-1's still in existence.

The Mid-Continent Museum bought one in 1963 for its scrap value, $2,400. The 1385 is now on the dead line at North Freedom, maybe never to steam again.

Another is privately owned but not restored and a third may be on static display out west somewhere. You'd think they could have saved at least one engine, a Class E-2 heavy Pacific that pulled the first 400 in 1935. So much for the C&NW's version of preserving our history and the romance of the railroads. The railroad was in terrible shape financially, but still. . . . The Robber Baron mentality still existed. In fairness, they were a little short of cash.

There were three classes of very large engines on the North Western; the Class J-4 Berkshires, 2-8-4's that were used mostly in the coal fields in southern Illinois, the Class H Northerns, 4-8-4's, used in freight and passenger service, and the Hudsons, 4-6-4 heavy passenger steam engines that had streamlining sheet metal. The Northerns got their name because the Northern Pacific ordered the first engine with that wheel arrangement. The North Western's Northerns were used primarily on the east-west main line from Chicago to Omaha, Nebraska, and from Chicago to Altoona via Milwaukee and the Adams cut-off. The H's were dual purpose engines, very capable in both passenger and freight service and some were

Don Ross collection

Class H-1 3011 spiffed up for Chicago Railroad Fair in 1948

balanced to run up to 90 miles an hour in passenger service. Engineers said they could handle a heavyweight twenty car passenger train without breaking a sweat. They were generally thought of as being among the most beautiful Northerns ever built. The North Western Northerns were big but not the heaviest of that class of engines built.

There were twelve J-4's and thirty-five class H's built in the 20's. The H's were way too heavy to run on the Madison Division line, as were the Berkshires. I saw an H-1 at the Chicago Railroad Fair in 1948 and another one once while I was working in Proviso Yard. I found out much later that the one I saw at the fair was the 3011 and the number I arbitrarily

Class H-1 3011 model

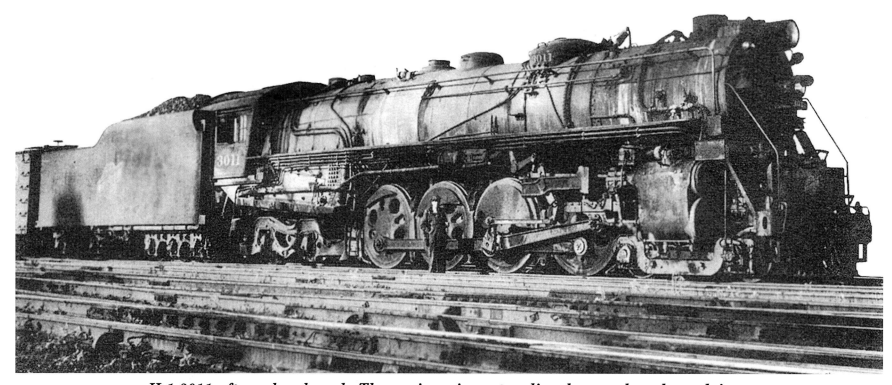

H-1 3011 after a hard week. The engine wiper standing by number three driver is trying to decide where to start.

selected when I bought a brass model many years later was the 3011. What goes around comes around. Engine 3011 was scrapped in 1954. I never did see a J-4, which was a handsome looking engine as seen in the pictures on pages 127 and 128. They looked very powerful but didn't have the grace of the H's.

One night I called the crew caller and asked him where I stood on the extra board.

The J-4 Berkshires were replaced in the southern Illinois coal fields by F covered wagons in the late 40's. The J-4's were then relegated to pulling general freight until they were scrapped in the early 50's.

He said I was first out and it looked like I'd be called for an extra out of Elroy in the morning. A circus train, but not the Great Circus Parade train out of Baraboo, was coming to Madison. In the morning our crew was in Elroy and picked up the train. For once, I was the senior brakeman and rode the wood bay-window caboose with the conductor, who had just recently been set up. This train was receiving special attention. Two railroad officials, the trainmaster and traveling engineer, were both riding the head end. The train consisted of passenger coaches on the front end for the performers and crew, then the cars carrying the animals, and finally a string of flat cars loaded with circus and concession stand wagons.

J-4 Berkshire working. After Ben Bass switched from engine wiper to trainman, clean engines apparently became a lesser priority on the C&NW.

Because of the circus animals and wagons we moved along at a fairly moderate speed, probably around forty miles an hour. We went past Baraboo and started down the grade past Devil's Lake and were getting close to the Merrimac Bridge. I was sitting on the right side of a bay window caboose. The conductor was on the left side at the conductor's table.

Looking through the front-angled window I saw a strange sight. A little way down the track were about six section men violently waving their arms and giving me wash-outs. As we approached they were throwing their tools in the air, their caps on the ground and shouting I couldn't tell what. This was high drama! I turned to the conductor and told him that something was wrong and we had to stop the train. He didn't move. He had recently been set up as a conductor and if he stopped the train unnecessarily he probably thought the officials and passengers would be very unhappy, and they would no doubt have been. I grabbed the conductor's trainline lever and dumped the air, putting the brakes into emergency stop. If the section guys are giving you wash-outs you know what you have to do, stop the train. The problem might have been a hot box, dragging brake rigging or a derailed set of trucks.

We got off the caboose and started down the road bed. I was a little ahead of the conductor and he'd not said a word. When we got farther down the track we saw the problem. The whole side of one of the wagons on a flat car, maybe the one that you try to knock down all the milk bottles in three tries, had swung down and was sticking straight out over the road bed. Apparently somebody forgot to drop a pin through a latch. Three or four of the circus guys who were riding on the flat cars with the wagons were just standing there. The railroad suits and circus officials arrived and looked the situation over. The roustabouts were told to swing the side of the wagon back up and latch it in place. There wasn't much said and I didn't hear any conversation about how the train got stopped. We all walked back to our respective ends of the train. No doubt everybody assumed that the conductor had dumped the air. As we proceeded down toward the bridge, which wasn't very far away, I tried to tell if the open side of the wagon would have hit an obstruction, like a signal tower along the tracks before or at the bridge. I couldn't tell.

Executive F7's heading the circus train at Monona Yard. The car knocker, kneeling, had probably just checked the train from the caboose to the engines.

The North Western's executive train power, F7's 402, 401, 400 and 403. Note that 402 has a Mars light.

used a number of different engines including the Wisconsin & Southern E9's and C&NW Geeps at various times. At least one year it used the North Western's four executive F7's. These units were used on the company business train that at various times ran over the system for inspections and promotional purposes. The trucks were painted silver which really dressed up the engines.

The Great Circus Train out of Baraboo ran every year for a number of years. It ran from Baraboo to Milwaukee with all personnel, animals, wagons, and equipment, stopping at various towns along the way. It also carried a large number of notables. It drew a lot of attention along the tracks and at grade crossings as it headed east. One year it was headed by the 1385 with a Geep behind the tender for insurance and maybe for a little help. The train

One of the runs I always enjoyed working was the sand job. At South Beloit there was a very large sand pit which is still active today. This was an unscheduled job and always ran as an extra. The five-man crew was junior men off the extra board. Like all trains not listed in the time table, the train number is always the number of the lead engine and flies two white flags or lights, one on each side of the front of the engine. An engine showing two green flags indicates the train is the first section of a regularly scheduled train. The second section shows no flags.

The train left Monona yard in the early evening pulling a string of empty open-top thirty-six foot hoppers. At DO siding in South Beloit we dropped off our empties on a side track, ran the engines back down to the end of our train, uncoupled our caboose and coupled it onto the back end of a string of loaded hoppers on another track. There were always two tracks of loaded hoppers to be picked up. Then we ran back up to the east end of the loads and pulled out the string that didn't have the caboose and put the train together. We made a brake test and headed for Harvard.

This was always a very heavy train because the sand was dripping wet, probably so it wouldn't blow away en route. Our power was always three GP7's and it seemed like they could just barely handle the train. Since the train was so heavy the engines were really working and it was a slow ride. There was a pretty good grade at Caledonia, Illinois, and we sometimes dropped down to five miles an hour but never had to double.

The GP7 normally operated up to 825 amps. This could be exceeded when starting a train and also for a specific length of time depending on how much over 825 amps the engine is operating. The generator is directly behind the cab and when the engineer starts to smell the varnish from the coils of an overheated generator it catches his attention.

This was all single track and we usually had a meet with 507, a passenger train that ran from Chicago to Madison via Beloit. Since our train was too long for the siding at the meet point, we had to saw by. The sand job headed into the siding and pulled down to the other end with the back part of the train still on the main. The sand job engine headlight was on bright to let 507's engineer know that the main was blocked. The passenger train would pull down to the west end of the siding. Then the head brakeman on the sand job opened the switch behind 507 and our train slowly moved out on the main. After the caboose cleared the main ahead of 507 the rear brakeman lined the switch for the main and 507 proceeded to Beloit.

We had to yard the train at Chemung Siding at Harvard, the end of our district and the beginning of the Wisconsin Division. The siding was on the west end of the yard and slightly uphill. If the train stopped for the brakeman to open the switch into the siding it probably couldn't get started so the brakeman dropped off the slow-moving train and ran for the switch, opened it and headed the train into the siding. So much for the rule that says no running on the railroad. Actually it wasn't critical for the brakeman to get the switch. If he didn't get to the switch in time to line it up the engineer would stop the train before the switch and double in if he couldn't get the train started. Not real high drama but close enough.

After the train was yarded, the engines were cut off and moved out on the main back to the depot. The conductor and hind brakeman walked up to the depot from the caboose and dropped off the waybills. There was a small restaurant on the north side of the depot so we went over to get something to eat, usually a piece of pie and a cup of coffee. Then back on the engines, west on the main, grabbed our caboose off the back of the sand train and headed non-stop back to Monona Yard. We were now what is known as a caboose hop, only engines and a caboose. Three big engines and a little red caboose made a strange sight.

A movement consisting of only engines and a caboose is called a caboose hop. An engine running with no cars is called a light engine. The crew on a light engine is only an engineer, fireman, and conductor. That move is usually made because the engine is needed somewhere else for a job or needs servicing. I never thought about it but somebody must have been keeping track of where all the engines were so there was always power in the right places for the right jobs.

Sand job extra 1601 caboose hop westbound from Harvard to Monona Yard

One night Dad and I caught the sand job. He, of course, was the conductor and I was the head brakeman. We had the usual tramp caboose, an old wooden one with a cupola. It was the usual run down to DO siding, drop off the empties, pick up the loads, yard the train on Chemung siding at Harvard, get something to eat, and head home. Instead of riding the engines I rode the caboose with dad and the rear brakeman rode the engines on the trip back to Madison. Most engineers had their own styles as to how they run their engines and our engineer, Tommy Vaughn, was not a slow poke. He liked to get over the road. Earlier he had been a fireman on an E-2 steam engine and had a collision with a Milwaukee Road engine that hadn't stopped for a red signal. His left hand was permanently damaged but functional. I had worked with him quite often. On this job we were paid by the mile, not time, so the sooner we got home the better. Tommy started out moving right along, going faster and faster.

The caboose was rocking and rolling pretty good but we were running on old 1890's passenger trucks and I wasn't too concerned. They were good riders. But Dad was getting pretty nervous. Then he got really agitated. Finally he pulled the air. Nothing. With three engines pumping air, the open train line in the caboose had no effect. Dad grabbed his lantern, went out on the back platform down to the

134

bottom step and wildly waved his lantern. Tom saw the light, literally, and slowed but dad was pretty shook up and not a happy conductor. There was no time for him to counsel with the engineer because as soon as the train got into the yard I cut off the engines and sent them down to the roundhouse as he was going to the yard office to register.

I had one unusual event on the sand job. We had a long string of empty hoppers going to DO. At Evansville the freight line branches off from the passenger line, a freight train short cut to Beloit that by-passed Janesville. I opened the switch and we moved through the switch, going slow so the hind brakeman could close it after the caboose went through and get back on the train. The track was curved and we couldn't see the back end so the engineer kept going slowly until he thought the caboose was through the switch and the brakeman was back on the train. This night he guessed wrong. The train had not cleared the switch when he throttled up and the rear brakeman couldn't catch the caboose. The conductor needed to stop the train. He gradually opened the train line valve on the back of the caboose. If you open the train line slowly it will not put the train into emergency stop but does start dragging the brakes on the back end of the train. Hopefully the engineer will see the air reduction on his gauge or feel the pull of the dragging brakes and stop.

But with the power of three engines and a string of empty cars we didn't feel any drag on the engines. With the engines pulling and the back end dragging, something broke and dynamited the brakes. We either busted a knuckle or much worse, pulled a drawbar. I walked back from the engines and the break was about two-thirds back. It was a busted knuckle and the resulting gap was a little over one car length long. I figured there were two ways to fix it. One was to go to the caboose and get a spare knuckle if it had one, stick a broom handle through the hole where the pin goes through it and the other brakeman and I would carry it up to the break. Those things are heavy so I decided to do it a lazy man's way. I went back up to the engine and threw off a knuckle.

I told the engineer I was going to set a twenty-minute fusee beside the cab, send him down the track and stop him when the last car of the break got up to me and the spare knuckle. Fusees will burn for ten minutes so you can get almost twenty minutes by lighting one, twist the top off the second one and set it at right angles to the burning fusee lying flat on the ground, about three-quarters of the way back from the flame. The lit fusee will burn down and light the second one.

The track ahead of the engine was straight so the engineer could see my signals. I had told him that I would stop him, load the knuckle on the back of the last car's coupler, set the fusees and give him a back-up signal. He should back up and stop at the fusees and wait. When we got the new knuckle installed I would dynamite the train line, letting him know we were done and he should pump off the brakes and slowly back up until he felt the coupling. Then he should stretch the train to make sure that both pins dropped, and wait. He did and the pins had dropped. I coupled up the air, walked up to the engine and we slowly moved ahead until the engineer was sure the rear guy was on the caboose this time. The knuckle busted because the engineer had increased the speed too soon for the rear brakeman to get on and in slowing down the train the conductor mismanaged the air line reduction, releasing too much air too fast.

Fusees went through a minor evolution. When I was working in '55 they had a long spike on one end. I'm not sure what the spike was to be used for. A brakeman on a caboose may drop a fusee if his train is slowing down but the odds of the spike sticking into a tie were less then remote. And it burned just fine lying down. The downside of carrying fusees in your pocket was that you occasionally got jabbed. Fusees came in ten- and five-minute sizes in the late 50's. By the end of the 50's the spikes were gone.

9

ONE evening I got a call from Jimmy West, the crew caller. He was ordering me out as the baggage man on heavy mail train 515 from Chicago, scheduled out of Madison at 12:10 a.m. I would have to work it from Madison to the Twin Cities. I told him the only experience I had in baggage cars was unloading parcel post for the Madison post office five or six years before. He knew I wasn't a qualified baggage car guy but said I was the only man available. Apparently the regular guy got sick or hurt and I was the only man on the extra board. I told him I'd never worked a baggage car before, at least not from the inside, and couldn't handle it. I couldn't talk Jimmy out of it and I knew I was in deep trouble. After a brief pause, Jimmy said if you don't go the train don't go. That was a pretty heavy load, and pretty much ended the conversation.

I reported that night. The guy I was relieving had a couple minutes to explain the job to me and then he was gone. I had to work at least two cars. I have blocked the actual number out of my mind. The cars had been loaded in Chicago and there was a pile of mail bags for each station to St. Paul which also included their surrounding towns, and the bags weren't located in stop sequence. In fact, adjacent towns might be in different cars. My job was to off-load the mail for each stop and take on their outbound mail. If any of the new mail was for stations farther up the line I was supposed to sort it in with that town's mail. Nobody was telling me this stuff. I was making it up as I went along. I had no idea where the mail for each town was located or in which car and not much time to find it. You had to read the mail bag tag to see what town it was going to. There were a few dozen stops and I had no idea where each station's mail was in the cars.

Since I had frequently worked the north end way freight, 563 and 562, At least I knew which side of the train the depots were on the way up to Elroy. After that, not a clue. At Elroy, one section of the train went west on the Omaha to Rochester and the one I was working went to Minneapolis. Unfortunately I still had the same number of cars after the split. And fortunately I was in one of the cars that went to St. Paul. Or unfortunately.

The trip started out bad and got worse. When I felt the brakes setting up I would look out each side of the train to see where the station was. The station agent was there but I usually didn't know where his mail was. Occasionally one would come aboard and find his mail. When I took his outgoing mail aboard I had no idea where to put it. To make matters worse the train crew was not real patient and didn't take kindly to any delays. And they weren't bashful about sharing their thoughts with me about how I was doing, or not. Past Elroy this crew was from another division and they had no idea who the yahoo was in the baggage car. Thank goodness. I might add that the station agents didn't seem too pleased about my performance either. People can be so impatient sometimes.

When we pulled into Minneapolis the baggage cars were disasters. I probably still had most of the mail that had been loaded in Chicago. And probably all the mail I had taken on board along the way and didn't know where to drop it off.

I was hot, sweaty and grimy when we arrived that morning. I skulked off the train and never having been there before had not a clue as to where the hotel was. I thought of asking somebody where to go but I didn't like the wording. I think I spotted an innocent looking clerk and got directions to the hotel. When I got there it had a grand entrance and I felt like a bum who'd just jumped off a freight. Apparently the railroad had an arrangement with the hotel for putting up train crews because the guy at the desk didn't throw me out or even give me a second look and assigned me a room. I would have thrown myself out.

After a not too restful night I had to deadhead back to Madison. I knew the regular baggage man going back was going to have a pretty big job unloading my unsorted and undelivered mail. I thought that since I had caused the problem I should probably work the job back with him and give him a hand. But I had a sense that this might be another guy that would like to tell me where to go. I was getting paranoid. So I deadheaded back to Madison hunkered down in the back of a half empty coach. The bottom line was that 515 had left Madison with only a token baggage man aboard. I think there were some comments made later but I never heard a word directly. Funny how

word can get back to Madison all the way from Minneapolis. And that was before e-mail.

Actually I had ridden a baggage car many years ago. Dad was working as a baggage man. His segment was from Madison to Chicago and he invited me to go along. It was a late Saturday run and naturally I thought that would be terrific and I was very excited.

Apparently some big Chicago newspaper had sent bundles of newspapers to Madison on an earlier train that were to be delivered by us on the way back to Chicago. My thought was that these Sunday morning papers were not dropped off going west because the depots on some stations were on the wrong side of the track for west bound trains and we would drop off the bundles for those stations going east. The interesting thing is that the train didn't stop at the stations the papers were going to, you simply kicked them off on the platform as the train went by. And the train didn't slow down. Dad opened the door about three feet and set the bundle at the opening. Then he stood behind it, looking down the track and at what he thought was the right moment, kicked the bundle out the door and hopefully onto the platform. There was some physics involved — velocity, wind speed, temperature, cohesion of a bundle of papers on brick platforms, bundle roll speed, and the like. Coming into Belvidere, Illinois, he asked me if I'd like to handle that drop. I thought I'd gone to heaven, and almost did. I was all pumped up, arms braced and ready to kick. I knew I had to push pretty hard because the bundle was probably a foot high. I looked out the door and when I saw the platform I went through all of the above mentioned calculations and gave a mighty kick. I went partially out the door and in that instant knew I was going to die. I had that feeling one other time in my life. On an aircraft carrier flight deck in the Pacific in some very nasty weather. But that's another story.

When we got to Chicago dad said we were going to the Forum, a new restaurant that had just opened which he had mentioned before after one of his trips. It sounded like big city stuff. We got there and it was brightly lit with a lot of stainless steel and very modern looking. There was a very long row of display cases with chrome rails running in front of them. The cases were full of serving size dishes. I had never seen anything like it. We grabbed trays and started down the line with its dazzling number of choices. It couldn't get any better than that.

I don't remember anything about the trip other than the two mentioned events but the Belvidere thing remains uppermost in my mind to this day. By far.

After braking on freights for a couple of years I was told I could work passenger trains. So I bought a passenger uniform and cap and was then eligible for both passenger and freight service working off the extra board. The transition from freight to passenger service was transparent, just the addition of a tail hose on the last car. A tail hose had a whistle on the end of it in case the train had to back over a crossing. The rear brakeman could also dynamite the train line in an emergency using the tail hose.

I wisely bought a wool winter uniform even though I worked more in the summer than winter because they looked better and held up very well. They were also hot as hell. In those days the air conditioning in the coaches was not real reliable. Navy blues were made of wool and about the same color and they held up pretty well so I figured I couldn't go wrong. The difference was that the Navy wisely switched to cooler whites in the summer. Apparently the railroads never thought of that.

Later I had another, better experience on 515. I was called for a job that I had to work from Elroy to Rochester as a trainman every day for two weeks. I was working off the freight board and got paid by the mile after a hundred miles. If you are in passenger service a basic day is 150 miles. If you are working off the freight board a basic day is 100 miles so for everything over that I was paid extra. That check was the biggest I ever got for two weeks' work. I think it was for $444.00.

It was an easy run. We were running on Omaha tracks and the rest of the crew were Omaha men. The Omaha track went west out of Elroy towards Rochester to Rapid City and beyond. Trains out of Chicago going to the Rochester Clinic had cars especially equipped to handle recumbent medical patients, sometimes accompanied by nurses or attendants. These cars had individual doors in the sides for easier patient loading and unloading. By this time most of that business had gone to planes and cars.

We probably got that job to equalize miles between railroads. For instance, if Omaha men ran so many miles on your line your men ran an equal number of miles on theirs. Fair is fair. Some interesting things happen on overnight trains but of course that's another story. It must be the uniform.

Train 515 left Elroy sometime after midnight and arrived at Rochester in the morning. I asked one of the guys where there was a good place to lay over and he suggested I wander around town and find a rooming house. On the first try I found one owned by a nice lady. The room was fine. Going back, I worked the train to Elroy and stayed on board deadheading to Madison. The next night I boarded 515 at Madison, deadheaded back to Elroy and worked the train to Rochester. I made about twice as much on that job as I needed for tuition for the next year at the University of Wisconsin. It probably even covered my books. I was also getting a monthly check under the GI Bill during the school year.

One day I caught an extra to the west end. That line ran from Madison to Montford, Fennimore and Lancaster. At that time the line also ran through Cuba City to Benton. Part of the line was a former narrow gauge railroad from southwestern Wisconsin to Platteville that serviced the lead mine part of the state in the very old days. It was a bucolic ride past rich farm lands and through lazy small towns, running on old sixty-five pound rail. A time warp back to the 1920's. The job was probably a west end turn, leaving Madison and going out to the end of the line to get stock cars of cattle and bring them back to Monona Yard. Part of the job this trip on the way back was to re-rail a box car that had gone on the ground, probably at Barneveld or Ridgeway.

When we got there I cut off our single engine and backed into the siding and coupled up to the de-railed box car. Two section men were there to get it back on the track. There was a re-railer to get cars back on the rails but that didn't work in this situation. The tops of the rails were at about ground level. The section guys had assembled various sized timbers and blocks and the idea was to arrange them in such a fashion that the wheel would climb the blocks and drop onto the rail. They'd rig a combination of wood blocking and when they said try it I'd give the engineer a slow go ahead. It didn't work. Try another combination. There's no right way to do it, just trial and error with the stuff you have.

This went on for probably twenty minutes and many tries. I was thinking of some possibilities that might do the trick but you didn't tell another man how to do his job, especially if he's been doing it for a long time and more especially in front of one of his peers and other guys, and even more so if you are a college man. Huge problem. What the hell. I said, try putting that piece there and this other one the other way, or something like that. I thought they might ignore me but by this time they were pretty exasperated and they did it. I gave a go-ahead to the engineer and the wheel rolled up and onto the rail. Very embarrassing. There would be no 'attaboy' today. Nobody said a word. I pulled the box car out of the siding and backed onto the train, climbed up on the engine and we went out of town leaving two section guys behind who were no doubt not very happy. Or did they appreciate what I did?

Nah!

Dad made his last run on train 531 in October, 1971, running from Lancaster to Madison. At that time the maximum speed on the line was 25 m.p.h. There were eight different locations on that track that had slow orders limiting the speed to ten miles an hour. Not long before, I had ridden his train from Lancaster back to Madison, spending most of my time on the engine, a chop-nosed Geep. I videotaped part of the trip. The engine motion was like riding through Monona Yard in the 50's, gently rocking and rolling. One unintended purpose the engine served was to keep down the

brush and branches that kept brushing the side of the train. That was probably much cheaper than using brush cutters.

Dad had a regulation set of horseshoes and stakes in a steel box that had been made for the set. He took it with him to Lancaster and apparently spent some of his time pitching horseshoes out there. I still have the set and for some reason it gets heavier every year.

I worked three passenger trains, 507 and 508 between Madison and Chicago, the Dakota 400 (518 and 519) between Madison and Winona and points west, and trains 514 and 515 from Elroy west to Rochester. In earlier days 507 and 508 had run from Chicago west through Elroy but by the mid 50's 508 originated at Madison and ran east to Chicago and 507 ran from Chicago to Madison. These trains ran as locals, making all stops between Madison and Harvard. Harvard was the western end of the North Western commuter district and 508 made a number of stops at the bigger suburban towns from Harvard to Chicago, as did 507 on the way back. The engine crews on these trains were always Wisconsin Division men, probably to equalize miles between their division and the Madison Division. Many of the commuter trains originated at Crystal Lake rather than Harvard.

One afternoon I had been ordered for 508 and when I got to the depot there wasn't much going on. The train was sitting on a side track.

A car knocker had probably turned on the air conditioning so the cars would be cool by the time we were scheduled out at about 5:30. I was usually the junior man, read flagman, on this train so I had to get the marker lights and fill the reservoirs with kerosene and take the air hose to the last coach, along with my overnight bag and flagging can.

Dakota 400 departing Madison depot for Chicago

144

The Dakota 400, 518, coming from Winona and points west, was probably on time, and arrived at the Madison depot at 5:10 p.m. She was scheduled to depart at 5:20, allowing ten minutes to unload and board passengers and luggage and test the brakes. Madison Division men crewed it from Winona to Madison and Wisconsin Division crews took it from Madison to Chicago. This train had the usual air brakes and was also equipped with electric brakes. Each system had to be tested separately, setting and releasing the brakes to make sure they both worked. The 400 made stops only at large towns. The train left Madison and would stop only at Evansville, Janesville and Beloit on its way to Harvard.

We did the brake test, loaded our passengers and followed them out of town about ten minutes later. Our headend power would be a covered wagon, an E7 or E8. Our passengers usually included three or four people who were going to places where the 400 didn't stop, Brooklyn and Oregon. Rather than take the 400 to Evansville, a lady regularly rode with us down to Evansville on Friday nights. There is a story there, must be something about uniforms, but anyway we left Evansville and are now high-balling to Janesville. The Janesville passengers would have taken the 400, so leaving Evansville we usually didn't have any revenue passengers, only the ones who might have gotten on at Brooklyn or Oregon and going to points east.

According to the time table we would have left Beloit at 7:23 p.m. heading out to DO Siding. It's an uphill grade going east past DO and when you reached the top there was very flat farm land and the track was fast. We could feel the train picking up speed and we were moving along pretty good. We had four cars at most and a large passenger engine which wouldn't be breathing very hard with this short train. I was sitting on the right side of the coach near the head end when bingo, the air went. You instantly know something bad has happened or will be happening. I looked out the window and saw a convertible at least twenty feet in the air, up and to the right and the heads of people inside. It was pointing due south, perfectly upright and stable and moving away. It looked like it had been an intentionally planned levitation. It was an astonishing sight and I was the only one who saw it.

When the train stopped the fireman climbed down off the engine and walked back toward us. We would wait for him, a perfect excuse for delaying our inevitable walk back to the wreck. He was the regular fireman and had a very freckled face. He was so pale I couldn't see his freckles. He said the car was racing the train. It was coming from the left side which is the fireman's side so he saw the whole thing as it developed, including the car disappearing under the nose of the engine and heard the crunch. An engine crew's worst nightmare.

As a group we started the long walk back to the car. Somehow I got ahead of the other guys and got to the site first. They managed to walk slower. It seemed like the next scene in a science fiction movie. The yellow Ford convertible was upright pointing in the same direction it had been going, sitting about fifty feet east of the highway and farther than that from the track. There were two guys and two girls, the driver was still in the car and the others were strewn around about ten or fifteen feet from the car. No movement, no blood and no twisted limbs. It was like they were just resting comfortably enjoying the evening sun. They were probably in shock. The back of the convertible was flattened from the rear right seat back to the left side of the back bumper. The only sound was the radio playing. It was incredibly surreal. Rod Serling couldn't have done it better.

Nobody was bleeding so I took off across the field toward the nearest farm house. A woman came out and shouted that she had called the sheriff's department. When I got back to the car one of the guys was trying to get up. He appeared to have a serious problem with his right leg and was all bent over. I went over to him and had him stay down on the ground. Still nobody said anything. Just the radio. By this time the rest of the crew had arrived.

The rescue people quickly got there and the conductor and fireman made their reports to the sheriff while the ambulance people picked up the victims. We got back on the train and headed for Harvard. The ironic thing was there were skid marks on the highway before the tracks. If the driver had kept going full speed he probably would have made it safely across the tracks. Another bet your life.

I'm pretty sure I know what happened to the car. The engine pilots on covered wagons slant forward and curve around the nose. At the speed the car was going its momentum was probably such that the impact and the angle of the pilot launched it into the air and it was going fast enough to keep pointing south. Or it did a 360 degree rotation. Don't try this at home. On the way back to Madison the next night on 507 we asked the station agent how badly the people were hurt. He said they were all O.K. I said what about the guy who seemed to have busted something. He said the guy had a disability and was just fine. The fireman had laid off this trip. Who could blame him?

I enjoyed catching 507 and 508 and worked that job fairly often. When we got to the Chicago terminal I had to take down the markers and tail hose and with my bag and flagging can walk down to the depot. This equipment was dusty and dirty and you're wearing your dark blue wool winter uniform. On a hot night in Chicago by the time you're done your J. C. Penney white shirt collar has sort of a limp grey appearance. Interestingly, later I would spend thirty-three years with the Penney company.

It was down to Chicago in the evening, and stay overnight at a fleabag hotel across from the depot. I think it cost about five bucks but hey, it had a great view of the magnificent Madison Street depot which no longer stands.

After checking in it was down to the Greek joint next door for a huge greasy Salisbury steak dinner. The place was dingy and had a high, dark ceiling, no doubt from grease from the grill over many years. Nick the Greek was the proprietor and looked the part. I'd guess he was either late first generation or early second. Very loud and colorful.

After supper, a short walk on the bridge over the Chicago River to enjoy the sights. The area, which usually has a lot of people coming and going, was totally empty after dark. Since the depot was right at the east end of skid row it also was not very safe at that time of night. One night a fireman got his throat cut, fatally, across from the depot. Those guys were very good at jack rolling people and knew all the moves. One night I met a guy on the bridge over the Chicago River and he asked for some money. He was short in stature but you never know. I declined his request and he kept bugging me. Finally I told him if he didn't leave I was going to throw him over the rail. He left. I probably shouldn't have been on the streets alone.

Going east past Harvard a number of regulars got on and went into the smoker. Four or five of them liked to play nickel dime poker going into Chicago. The conductor often had a small board, usually with a whiskey ad on it. He also brought the cards. The guys would pull up

Northwestern Station Chicago, Illinois

chairs and let the game begin. They would pull a dime out of each pot for the conductor for bringing the board and cards. It must have been pretty profitable because about that time dad bought an old black Cadillac as a second car.

148

50's 508 crew, from left — Wisconsin Div. fireman;
Chalfant, trainman; Roy Hubbard, flagman;
Al Hillebrandt, engineer; Roger Bass, conductor

Roger Bass, conductor; Roy Hubbard, flagman;
Chalfant, trainman; Al Hillebrandt, engineer

Roger Bass, conductor, Chalfant, trainman

Conductor Roger Bass
and retired conductor Ben Bass

Bill Martin, trainmaster; Roy Hubbard, flagman; Ben Bass; Roger Bass, conductor; Jorgenson, stationmaster. Jorgenson was a man of vision. He hired me for the clerk's job in 1950

I liked poker and played a lot in the Navy but was pretty busy calling stations and loading and unloading passengers. The suburban Chicago stops were fairly close together. After I gave a highball I'd go in the smoker and play cards, standing up. When I felt the brakes setting up for the next stop I called the station, opened the trap and stopped the train where the passengers on the platform had congregated. If I had the

beginnings of a decent hand I'd tell the guys to keep me in and do the unload and load thing. When I got back I'd see how I had done. They were a pleasant bunch and it was very enjoyable, if not exactly according to company policy. But the suits should be home for dinner.

If there had been an official on board I would have reminded him that there was a precedent, at least for passengers playing cards. The new

Marker lights, cardboard and cards, Dad's lantern and the author's flagging can, all used on trains 507 and 508

streamlined 400's that went into service in 1939, one going each way, had two card tables in each of their observation or tail cars. These were first class passenger cars so we were simply continuing an old tradition, albeit a poor man's version, and improving customer relations. I'm sure he would have understood. Does anybody believe that?

Stopping at each station, the brakeman has to lean out of the trap to see the platform and the waiting people and stop the train accordingly. The train was on a tight schedule so the starts and stops are made as fast as possible. With the brakes set, a lot of dust and steel is thrown up. I always wore gloves in passenger service and before each stop I usually grabbed a paper towel from the rest room and wiped down the hand rails and grab irons. The passengers appreciated that because these things got pretty grimy between stops.

One night I got an eye full of debris while signaling a stop. I was very uncomfortable the next morning so I went to the company surgeon in Chicago. He looked at my eyes and sent me to an ophthalmologist. He looked at my eyeballs and said they looked like battlefields and said it had no affect on my vision. One eye was O.K. but he had to pick stuff out of the other one with a needle. He actually spent quite a bit of time doing it. He gave me a tube of salve and a black eye patch and sent me on my way. I had all day in Chicago and was scheduled to go out on 507 that night.

In the evening you hung the marker lights and hooked up the signal hose. The good part is that the back end of the train is now at the terminal entrance and not much walking was involved. When the engine was put on the train you made the brake test, and when the train number and destination is called, loaded the passengers. Since this was the start of the run we always left on time. After leaving the station a running brake test had to be made. After getting up some speed the engineer set the train's brakes, slowing it down. When the rear brakeman heard the brakes and felt the train slowing down he gave a long pull on the signal chord to let the engineer know that the brakes on the last coach were working. When he got the brakeman's signal he released the brakes and we were on our way out of town. Pulling the signal chord blew a little air whistle in the engine cab.

Leaving the depot, the view from the back platform was an impressive sight — the huge Merchandise Mart, tall buildings and the skyline outlined by a bright orange color. One night I was really enjoying the view when I noticed that we seemed to be going slower and slower, almost at a stop. My worst fear was we were going to stop and I'd have to get off and flag. Leaving the Madison Street terminal you are literally in the middle of acres of rails and switches, all electrically operated ready to clamp an unwary brakeman's ankle. I finally realized that the engineer was waiting for the brake signal! The good news is the brakemen on passenger trains don't usually see the engine crew, at least not that night. Also the conductor and head brakeman didn't have any comments. Maybe they thought I was being overly conscientious or they didn't notice.

My eye incident was reported to Madison. Railroads, especially the North Western, were very safety-conscious. Any accident that resulted in missed work had to be reported to the Federal Railroad Administration and the railroads didn't like that. It looked bad in their accident statistics. The next day the crew caller, Jimmy West, called and asked if I would go out on 508 that night. I think he thought I wouldn't go. I said sure and the suits were pleased that they wouldn't have to report the eye problem as a missed work injury. I went out, eye patch and all that afternoon.

Coming out of Chicago 507 was pretty well loaded. A lot of people stayed in town for the evening or worked late. The regular commuters had a pre-paid badge they wore on their jackets or ties showing the station where they get off. At one stop a young lady was getting off. In those days people dressed very well. She was wearing high heels and as she stepped off the trap platform her heel caught and she pitched forward right out of the trap. I caught her as she went flying by and set her down. She was really rattled and spent a moment getting her bearings. Then she turned and walked away. No thanks you's, no telephone number. Not even an over-the-shoulder smile as she

William F. Armstrong

North Western – Milwaukee Road interlock plant west of the C&NW depot

disappeared into the night. Helping passengers was in my job description but how about saving somebody's life? What a thankless job. She had to be in shock. Serious shock.

Not only was the train loaded but so were some of the passengers. A lot of them were just plain tired. Before each stop the train crews called the station and woke up passengers for that station who had fallen asleep. The trainmen could tell by their passes where they were supposed to get off. One night a guy was sleeping really well. I woke him up for his station and after we left the station I noticed he was still aboard. I woke him up and mentioned that he had missed his station. That caught his attention. The next stop was about a twenty minute ride by taxi, or about an hour by wife. He was very unhappy. And she was going to be.

One of the better jobs for me was working the Dakota 400 from Madison to Winona, Minnesota, again at freight pay. By this time there weren't very many passengers and it was a pleasant run. The train came in from Chicago manned by a Wisconsin Division crew. The marker lights and tail hose would go through

so we didn't have to handle that. We did have to make the usual brake tests, one for the air brakes and one for the electric brakes. Streamlined trains all had electric brakes and passenger engines were all equipped with the controls to operate them.

Electric brakes were not as powerful as air brakes but they worked well going over the road. When the train reached about 30 miles an hour the engineer had the option of switching from air brakes to electric brakes. At speed, the engineers liked them because they were faster acting than air brakes and that gave them better control. When the train slowed down to 30 miles an hour the engineer switched back to air brakes. He needed those more powerful brakes for positive stopping. The two systems did not work in parallel. The train was on one or the other but not both. Worst case — an engineer failed to switch to air brakes coming into a terminal and ran through it.

We stopped only at Baraboo, Reedsburg, and Elroy. From there we proceeded to Winona through the tunnel district which is now a hiking and biking trail. When we got to Winona another crew took over the train, made their brake tests, and went out of town, going to Huron, South Dakota, and later only to Rochester, Minnesota. I would grab a bunk upstairs in the depot and the next day work 518 back to Madison.

Jim Neubauer

Dakota/Rochester 400 westbound past North Freedom

155

Going east the Dakota 400 met the Twin Cities 400 at Wyeville. Their passengers going to towns on the old line transferred to our train and our passengers going down the new line to Milwaukee and beyond transferred to their train. That meet would have made a great picture.

The Milwaukee Road tracks paralleled the North Western's for a few miles on that route. One day we were moving pretty fast eastbound and the Hiawatha had overtaken us, running quite a bit faster than we were. They had better track. Then their wheels turned into brilliant orange circles of fire. It was a beautiful sight. The train must have applied their emergency brakes or made a very heavy brake line reduction for stopping at Wisconsin Dells, with spectacular results. Oh, for a camera.

One year National Guard troops were moving from Illinois and Indiana to Camp McCoy by Pullman sleepers through Milwaukee for their two-week summer encampment. The Wisconsin Division crewed them to Milwaukee and we took them to Camp McCoy, now called Fort McCoy. I was called to report to the Milwaukee depot to crew one of these trains. There were a number of them, long trains with the old heavyweight dark green Pullman sleepers manned by Pullman porters. When I got there I was immediately assigned as flagman on a train standing at the station ready to go. It had just come in from Chicago and the marker lights and tail hose were in place so all I had to do was get on board. A fellow Madison Division man, Freddie Siles, Hank's son, was the head brakeman. I don't recall making the usual brake test. Somewhere in the mix there had to be a conductor but I don't recall seeing him. There were no tickets to be taken. We left the station and headed out on the new line toward Adams.

I had never been on the new line but that didn't make much difference working this troop train. It was a straight shot from Milwaukee to Camp McCoy making no stops. I had a timetable which indicated where the control towers were on the line. The men in these towers always watch trains going by and if everything looks all black they give a highball to the flagmen on the back of the train, who acknowledges in kind. All's well. All railroad employees are expect to watch passing trains and give a highball to the flagmen. Now, since there is nobody on the rear of trains, if there is a problem they have to call somebody. Modern technology gives the engine crews most of the information they need to operate their trains safely. FRED, Flashing Rear End Device, had replaced the caboose. Just for old time's sake they should hang a caboose on the back end of all freights. Every sentence needs a period.

We got to Camp McCoy and unloaded the troops. There was another now-empty train there so they combined the two and made one very long, heavy, empty train with four engines on the head end, E7's and/or E8's. Somehow I wound up as the flagman again. It was very dark and I didn't feel like I was connected to anything or anybody, just isolated. The engine headlight was a dim glow on the horizon. No brake tests, static or running, were made that I know of. On a train that long the whistle cord used to signal the engineer was useless. The head guy who I found out later was again

Freddie Siles, may have made a brake test on the head end cars to see if they worked on that end but I wasn't in the mix. Our train was on a siding so I knew I'd have to close the switch on the main line after we went through it. I stood around and finally the train started to move. Did anyone know I was back here or did they go on faith? Did anybody care? I didn't hear the engineer whistle a highball but the train started to move. Fortunately the train was moving very slowly and I figured if the engineer kept up this speed I could close the switch and get on board. He did and I did. I got a fusee, lit it, and threw it as high in the air as I could. Apparently somebody up front noticed and the speed picked up immediately. I didn't hear the engineer whistle a response but he probably did.

I closed the trap, walked into the car and heard low voices. What's this? I thought I was alone. People were talking in a closed compartment. I opened the door and there was a group of Pullman porters sitting around smoking and chatting. All conversation stopped as they looked at me. I really felt like an intruder, said hey, and backed out and closed the door.

Pullman cars were owned by the Pullman Company and leased to the railroads, complete with all necessary supplies and equipment. The porters were Pullman employees, carefully selected by the company and well trained in their jobs. Very dark men were preferred. It apparently had to do with keeping distance between the races, which wasn't always successful. Each man had one car and the Pullman conductor in charge of their cars was always white.

These men were very territorial, their cars were their domain. Train crews had very little to do with them and vice versa. They loaded and unloaded their passengers. In the course of our duties we had to pass through their cars but they weren't real pleased to see us. These men enjoyed high status in their communities since being a porter was a pretty good-paying job and they were widely traveled. They learned the ways of upper class whites and were important conduits of white culture back to black communities. Black barber shops were a good source for news and porters had some interesting stories to tell.

Passengers brought papers and magazines aboard and when they were left behind, the porters took them home or threw them off their trains at selected locations along the line in black communities. Pullman porters were the backbone of the black middle class. In the early part of the twentieth century their union became quite strong and their union leaders were key players in the birth of the NAACP.

When our engines stopped at the depot in Milwaukee I was still out in the country. I saw the approaching headlights of another train and as it went by I saw Freddie, our head brakeman. He had gotten off our train and onto another one waiting for crewmen and was waving to me with a big smile. He was making another round trip and some serious money and I wasn't. There were no trains left when our last car finally pulled up to the depot. Oh well.

10

THE Jefferson Junction switch run was a job that I caught only a few times. It's where the line from Fond du Lac to Janesville, the Lakeshore Division, crossed the line from Madison to Milwaukee. It has huge grain storage silos, the largest such facility in the world until a larger one was built in Belgium a few years ago. It is used to hold barley coming in by rail from the west. They converted barley to malt and shipped the malt to major beer makers.

Switching the junction is an all day job, lining up loaded cars of barley to be dumped and pulling malt cars out for shipping to the breweries. In the 50's the grain came in boxcars which were not easy to unload. These were usually old cars and a lot of them were leakers. Who knows how many bushels of barley were lying on the roadbed of thousands of miles of track.

Each box car was moved individually into the malt house and one of its doors opened. The car was then rolled partially on its side and rocked fore and aft, dumping the grain. Don't ask me how, I never saw it done. Today covered hoppers with hatches that open under the cars are used to dump the grain. It was a pretty busy place, shoving loads of barley into the malt house and pulling the empties out. At the same time you're pulling loads of malt out and making up trains going to various locations. And new loads of barley were coming in every day.

Ladish Grain Silos at Jefferson Junction

At one time it was a very busy place for passenger trains as well. The depot was built on an angle, part of it parallel with the Madison–Milwaukee line and part parallel to the Fond du Lac–Janesville line. Passengers would transfer from north-south to east-west trains and vice versa. There was a fine old restaurant in the southwest quadrant of the the track called the Maximillian House. For passengers making connections and the locals, it was a good place to eat. Sometime later, after the golden age of passenger service ended I spent an evening there, a Friday night fish fry, and it was showing its age. Today nothing remains. It burned down. The days of gracious dining at Jefferson Junction are gone, as is the depot. In 2007 a very large ethanol plant was built at the Junction and is now converting corn to ethanol.

North Western switching the
⇦ *Jefferson Junction malt plant*

The Maximillian House appears behind the depot. Both mainlines, Madison-Milwaukee and Janesville-Fond du Lac were still open. The Madison line shows red order boards.

The winter of 1958 was very snowy and the plows were out. That was during the winter months during which I laid off to go to school. The following pictures were taken on the Madison west end and on track north of Elroy to Kendall. I worked with all the guys in the pictures but unfortunately don't remember all of their names.

Tom Vaughn, fireman; second from left, Ron Caves, engineer; fourth, Roger Bass, conductor; fifth, Bill Martin, trainmaster; right, Ted Barcio, roadmaster

Second from left, Donny Kopp, brakeman; third, Ron Caves, engineer; sixth, Ted Barcio, roadmaster; far right, Roger Bass, conductor

Roger Bass, conductor; second from left, Kenny Ellestad, brakeman; third, Don Tobias, brakeman; fourth, Tommy Vaughn, engineer; kneeling, Chuck Juve, fireman

162

Second from left, Bill Martin, trainmaster;
third, Tommy Vaughn, fireman;
far right, Ron Caves, engineer

Cobb on the west end

Kendall west of Elroy

During the 50's and 60's the North Western, which had always been known for their frugal ways, bought a number of used engines from whoever was selling. They collected a number of used engines from other railroads and over time overhauled them or re-engined them, as they did to the ones they had originally bought new. They even bought four E's with no cabs and an engineering department guy named Crandall built his version of cabs on them. They weren't very pretty but they did the job.

When I received my degree in economics from the University of Wisconsin, I felt that all the pieces had come together. I had railroad operating experience plus a pretty good understanding of how the world of business works. My goal was still to become a Railroad Robber Baron. I got an interview with the railroad's vice president of operations and went to the Chicago depot and up into the eagle's nest, with its dark paneled walls, carpeted floors and heavy wooden doors.

The vice president was not a real warm, cordial guy. He appeared to be well on his way to becoming a Robber Baron himself. We had a brief discussion, going over my resume and experience and he allowed that he could probably offer me a position as an assistant trainmaster out in Iowa, which was on the main line of the railroad from Chicago to Omaha. Probably not a bad place to start, a lot of action out there. Trainmasters often came up through the ranks but I felt with a degree, I needed to start at a higher level than that. I had already paid some dues. I declined his kind offer, thanked him for his time and headed back to Madison. Much, much later it occurred to me that the only job an operations guy could offer was a job in operations. I should have started with the personnel department.

On the drive back to Madison I decided my fallback was to become a Captain of Industry. Someone suggested that a degree in engineering would serve me better for that and perhaps with my degree in economics I would be best suited to enter the World of Commerce. So that's what I chose to do.

My first job was in Chicago working as an industrial engineer for Wards. At the end of most weeks I went back to Madison and reported on the extra board. The crew caller, Jimmy West, knew that I could only work weekends so I would catch jobs like the Dakota 400, out Saturday and back Sunday, or a west end stock turn or some other Saturday or Sunday extra. Sunday night I'd lay off and go back to my day job in Chicago. It couldn't get any better than that.

This wasn't going to last forever. There had always been grumbling in the ranks from guys who were hired after me. Because I had hired out before I joined the Navy, the railroad had to give me a leave of absence to go to school under the G.I. Bill and maintain my seniority. If any of the guys that had less seniority than I did had served in the military I wasn't aware of it. I had paid my dues, four years worth.

I took off in the fall and reported back in the spring with another year's seniority. Not only that but during Thanksgiving, Christmas and spring vacation I'd report back on the extra board. A lot of the regular guys wanted off for the holidays and Jimmy was glad to have me available and I was happy to get the work. After college classes were over in the spring I worked steady all summer.

Actually I never did take a leave of absence from the time I started with the railroad to the end of my service. I just never reported for work while I was in the Navy and just laid off and reported to the extra board while I was in school. Most times I reported I'd get jobs off the extra board. I'd report during Christmas or spring vacation and then lay off until I had another break that I could work.

400 at Merrimac eastbound for Madison

To qualify for Railroad Retirement you had to work at least one day a month in 120 months, ten years service. I hadn't worked at least one day for 120 months. Had I known, I would have reported on weekends while I was in college and would have probably gotten the months needed. My earned Railroad Retirement was rolled into Social Security.

My working only on weekends was just too much for the junior guys. This had been going on for a few months and the trainmaster, Charlie Cook, was getting heat. Finally he told Jimmy that the next time I laid off I was done. Jimmy told him I was his ace in the hole and would work when nobody else was available or wanted to work. No dice. I reported on a Friday evening and was ordered for the Dakota, now Rochester 400, the next day. Jimmy told me when he ordered me that if I laid off when I got back I was done. I savored the trip, knowing it would be my last.

When I returned to Madison Sunday afternoon I pulled the pin. I stepped off 518 and took my flagging can and lantern and walked off the property. There couldn't have been a better last run than being the flagman on the 400. It was a good run and a great last trip. And it was the end of the era of iron men and wooden cabooses. But I'm still waiting for a call from Jimmy West. The 400 was taken out of service less than a year later.

11

TRAINS run on the shiny iron but they need paper to do it, or at least they did while I was working. The required paperwork was CLEARANCE FORM A, authorized by the chief train dispatcher. Along with the clearance, they usually received train orders.

Employee time tables show all permanent speed limits and other restrictions that train crews are normally expected to observe. After the time tables are published speed limits and restrictions may change for a number of reasons, most of which are usually temporary. For example, speeds may be reduced for a section of bad track which will probably be repaired at some later date.

Train crews may receive orders at any station on their runs where there is an operator on duty. These may be orders from the dispatcher who has received information the crew needs after they have left their terminal. They can be given to the train crew "on the fly" without the train having to stop. Each operator had a few sticks that formed a Y on one end. He'd tie the train orders with a string loop which he'd stretch into a triangle by attaching the loop to a friction point on each corner of the Y. When the engine and caboose pass by, the operator holds the stick up beside the train and an engine crewman and a man in the caboose each run a fist through the loop, capturing the train orders. One operator had a stick with a curved closed loop at the end and attached the orders to the loop. The train crewman had to hook the loop, remove the orders and throw the stick on the ground as quickly as possible. The longer he took the farther the operator had to walk to retrieve his stick. A couple of those sticks with a Y might have saved him some steps.

168

NOTICE

Pursuant to notices filed with the Interstate Commerce Commission, the following trains will make their last trips as follows:

No. 507   Chicago-Madison   Sun., Sept. 5, 1965

No. 508   Madison to Chicago   Sun., Sept. 5, 1965

No. 510   Madison to Chicago   Fri., Sept. 3, 1965

CHICAGO AND NORTH WESTERN RAILWAY

Notice of the last Chicago & North Western passenger service at Madison

Roger Bass was the conductor of the last scheduled North Western passenger train out of Madison. It left Chicago on Saturday, September 4, 1965, from the Madison Street depot as 507 and returned to Chicago as 508 on Sunday, September 5. Two clearances were required for each trip. Following are the clearances for those two trips.

Form 1 (top left)

Form 200   100M 8-64

Chicago and North Western Ry. Company

A   **CLEARANCE FORM A**   **A**

SEP 4 1965   19____

To C & E _No 507_   AT _CHICAGO_

I have _7_ orders for your train.
(If no train orders, operators must write "No" in space provided above.)

No. _670_ No. _657_ No. _656_ No. _654_ No. _650_ No. _648_ No. _655_

Orders: No.____ No.____ No.____ No.____ No.____ No.____ No.____

No.____ No.____ No.____ No.____ No.____ No.____ No.____

This form is authority to pass Train Order signal at Stop indication.

Block _____ Do not leave before _____ M (Rule 91)

Time _901 P_ M OK _GEM_ _____ _Racko_
       Chief Train Dispatcher   Operator

When block is not clear, the line giving block indication will specify what permissive forms have been issued in addition to Clearance Form A.
(See Rules 211 and 318)

Train 507 cleared from Chicago to Harvard

Form 2 (top right)

Form 200   1 MM 9-63

Chicago and North Western Ry. Company

A   **CLEARANCE FORM A**   **A**

Sept 5   19_65_

To C & E _No 508_   AT _Madison_

I have _3_ orders for your train.
(If no train orders, operators must write "No" in space provided above.)

No. _652_ No. _643_ No. _642_ No.____ No.____ No.____ No.____

Orders: No.____ No.____ No.____ No.____ No.____ No.____ No.____

No.____ No.____ No.____ No.____ No.____ No.____ No.____

This form is authority to pass Train Order signal at Stop indication.

Block _____ Do not leave before _____ M (Rule 91)

Time _559 P_ M OK _GEM_ _____ _Hansen_
       Chief Train Dispatcher   Operator

When block is not clear, the line giving block indication will specify what permissive forms have been issued in addition to Clearance Form A.
(See Rules 211 and 318)

Train 508 cleared from Madison to Harvard.
The operator who wrote the order was Doug Hansen,
who was well-known and liked by everybody.

Form 3 (bottom left)

Form 200   1MM 5-65

Chicago and North Western Ry. Company

A   **CLEARANCE FORM A**   **A**

To C & E _No 507_   _September 4_ 19_65_   AT _Harvard_

I have _4_ orders for your train.
(If no train orders, operators must write "No" in space provided above.)

No. _652_ No. _643_ No. _642_ No. _107_ No.____ No.____ No.____

Orders: No.____ No.____ No.____ No.____ No.____ No.____ No.____

No.____ No.____ No.____ No.____ No.____ No.____ No.____

This form is authority to pass Train Order signal at Stop indication.

Block _____ Do not leave before _____ M (Rule 91)

Time _1109 P_ M OK _GEM_ _____ _Shinskie_
       Chief Train Dispatcher   Operator

When block is not clear, the line giving block indication will specify what permissive forms have been issued in addition to Clearance Form A.
(See Rules 211 and 318)

Train 507 cleared from Harvard to Madison

Form 4 (bottom right)

Form 200   1MM 5-65

Chicago and North Western Ry. Company

A   **CLEARANCE FORM A**   **A**

To C & E _No 508_   _Sept 5_ 19__   AT _Harvard_

I have _4_ orders for your train.
(If no train orders, operators must write "No" in space provided above.)

No. _672_ No. _670_ No. _648_ No. _635_ No.____ No.____ No.____

Orders: No.____ No.____ No.____ No.____ No.____ No.____ No.____

No.____ No.____ No.____ No.____ No.____ No.____ No.____

This form is authority to pass Train Order signal at Stop indication.

Block _____ Do not leave before _____ M (Rule 91)

Time _826 P_ M OK _GEM_ _____ _Operator_

When block is not clear, the line giving block indication will specify what permissive forms have been issued in addition to Clearance Form A.
(See Rules 211 and 318)

Train 508 cleared from Harvard to Chicago

Each of these clearances came with multiple train orders. Order 635 is one example and was included in both the eastbound and westbound clearances between Harvard and Chicago on these trips. Sometimes the train order shows the reason the order was issued. In this case the reason for the order is unknown. There were a total of seventeen train orders for this round trip.

Train order

Now there were no passenger trains back to Madison so dad had to find another way to get home. According to his deadhead slip he left Chicago at 7:30 Monday night and arrived in Madison at 4:00 Tuesday morning, a very long night. He may have deadheaded home on time freight 591.

Deadhead slip from Chicago to Madison after the last passenger run

Somehow the marker lights of 507 and 508 wound up in the trunk of dad's car. His thinking probably was "no train, no markers needed." These lights, which are pictured on another page, were almost new and have long range fuel tanks in them which I had never seen before.

Sunday, September 5th, 1965, 508 at Monona Yard in Madison about to make its last revenue run to Chicago. Note that the baggage and passenger cars are not in their usual sequence. Dad may have boarded the train in the yard rather than at the depot so his car would be in the yard when he deadheaded back on freight 591. He is standing beside the engine.

Conductor Roger Bass and engineer Jim Butterfield — last run for 508

C. AND N. W. RY. CO. MADISON DIV

DISPATCHER'S RECORD OF MOVEMENT

TIME TABLE NO. 8

PLACE *Madison Wis* DATE *Thu*

The dispatcher's register shows Roger Bass as conductor of the east end way freight 679, lead engine GP7 1524. The consist for passenger trains 601 and 620, Madison to Milwaukee and return, on the bottom of the sheet [not shown] was mail car 8127, baggage car 8751, and passenger car 6125. Head end power was unit 5005A, an E7 or E8.

The **DISPATCHER'S RECORD OF MOVEMENT OF TRAINS** sheet showed Dad as the conductor of way freight 679 going from Milwaukee to Madison on Thursday, February 8, 1956. They spent two hours switching at Jefferson Junction and fifty-three minutes at Deerfield, probably for switching and breakfast. He tied up at Monona Yard at 9:15, eight hours and forty-five minutes on duty. He would often go home and then go to work as a journeyman electrician for a local contractor. He worked too many long days.

173

After I left the railroad I had a continuing interest in railroading. Dad would work another ten years so we'd chat about the happenings on the railroad.

Interesting things can come up more than fifty years after they happened. At a C&NW Veterans Association breakfast recently I was sitting across from an engineer, Al Blood. He asked me if I remembered the time our engine lost power on the road and I found the problem. The engine crew figured it was a blown cartridge fuse but the fuse tester on the engine was missing or broken. He said I took the battery out of my lantern and unscrewed a light bulb, did a continuity check of the fuses and found the bad one. I now vaguely remember that. I had been an electrician in the Navy.

Dad had an interesting if unfortunate experience at Jefferson Junction in 1962, the year after I left the railroad. He was ordered for a Butler turn to pick up a block of cars at Butler and set out eighteen of them, mostly barley, at the Junction on the return trip. Before he left Monona Yard he was told to stop at the Junction on the way over and check for a clear track to set out those cars coming back, which would be after dark.

The train number of unscheduled trains, extras, is the number of the lead engine, which shows two white lights or white flags on the front of the engine. The lead engine was GP7 1645, the first of three units. At Jefferson Junction the engineer made the mandatory stop as all trains do at the diamond where the Lake Shore line crosses the Madison Sub. None of the train crew got off and made a thorough check of the status of the tracks. This was during daylight. That was mistake number one.

They came out of Butler Yard late that night with 96 cars, a heavy train. The long and short of it was they cut off the eighteen cars to be set out and made a blind shove on a track that they thought was empty. That was mistake number two. The track was the North Mill which feeds the car dump. Actually there were twelve loads of barley on that track. Remember the book of rules, Rule 103? You can make a blind shove only in switch yards.

There was a derail on the North Mill track just before the unloading unit. The knuckles on both the lead car in the shove and the first car in the string standing on that track were closed so on impact the twelve rolled, two of which ran over the derail and went on the ground. Then the cars ran into the mill house and busted up the unloader. The impact cracked the draw bar pocket on engine 1645, which was now the trailing unit.

The transcript of the disciplinary hearing is 58 pages long and very interesting. I knew all the players. Their answers to the question as to the speed at impact varied from 8-12 miles an hour, walking speed, 3-4 miles an hour, and "I couldn't tell." A maximum of four miles an hour was suggested for coupling up. Dad got time off but was paid by the Brotherhood of Railroad Trainmen's union during that duration. I don't know how long it was. The assessment in 1964 was $3.96 a month. Benefits were $12.00 per

day. That's $80.00 in today's dollars. Since he was also a journeyman electrician he did that work during his time off and probably made more money than he would have on the railroad. Incidentally, the trailing engine going eastbound was the 1518 so coming back it was the lead engine and the train was extra 1518, the North Western's first GP7. The bottom line is one of the crew should have made sure the north mill was clear or the hind brakeman should have been on the point of the shove. In any case the conductor was responsible.

Dad had another interesting experience on what must have been the north end way freight, 563. In the cut at Okee between a country store and highway 113 his train went on the ground. The train was a little over a mile from the Merrimac bridge that crosses the Wisconsin River.

Wreck at Okee, February, 1968

The sixteenth car from the engines derailed and took ten more cars off the tracks with it, about half of them TOFCs, trailers on flat cars, also known as piggy-backs. The

Wreck at Okee, February, 1968

probable cause was a broken rail. None of the crew were hurt and nobody was responsible for the accident. These photos were taken by conductor Roger Bass at the time of the accident.

The strength of a rail is compromised by the two holes in each end that are needed to connect the rails together. The rails are connected together by a rail joint called a fish plate, a bar with four holes, two through each end of each rail. A fish plate is used on both sides of the joint.

Fish plates or rail connecters on both sides of the rail joint hold the rails together. A wire is welded at each rail joint to ensure good electrical conductivity. The ballast is Pink Lady quartzite from the quarry at North Freedom, WI.

If rails are going to break it's usually at a bolt hole where the strength of the rail is weakest. Today a lot of track is continuous welded rail, eliminating most of the broken rail problem. The down side of welded rail is in extremely hot weather it can expand and distort the rail. I talked to a section guy who said his partner could tell a bad joint as he drove his Hy-Railer over it by the sound of it. Guess I'm not sure about that one. A Hy-Railer is a street vehicle that has four small flanged boggy wheels that permit the vehicle to ride on rails and are retractable for highway driving. The vehicle's tires ride on the rails and provide the propulsion. The vehicles used are usually equipment trucks or SUV's. Railroads have rail inspection cars used for detecting bad rails which were operated over the system periodically.

12

IN **1964** my brother John and his wife, who had horses, decided they needed a tack room and an old caboose would work perfectly. They had a home in the country with plenty of room. Dad found a caboose for sale in Green Bay and the North Western would move it to Monona Yard free. It was an old wood cupola caboose in pretty good shape. In the course of cutting off the hardware beneath the caboose it caught fire and was destroyed. Green Bay had another caboose that wasn't in very good shape and the cupola had been removed. They moved it to Monona Yard and John hired a trucker to pick it up and deliver it to his property outside Verona. Total cost was about $60 to the North Western plus trucking costs. The railroad would not sell the trucks and the steps had to be removed to set it on the ground. It was set on rail ties so the platforms were about one step above the ground.

The caboose, 11546, had been built in May, 1915, and underwent no modifications except for the removal of its cupola when it went through the Chicago Shops for refurbishing in the late 20's. Over time trains got longer and faster and cabooses were subject to more rough handling as the coupler slack between cars ran in and out, which resulted in higher maintenance. Since the trucks had wood frames they needed more maintenance than newer steel trucks.

In the spring of 1999 John and I looked at the caboose and he said he thought he might burn it and sell the steel as scrap. The horses were long gone and it was looking pretty sad. I knew the value of a caboose, if for nothing more than its sentimental value. Besides, where are we going to get another one like that? Our father and grandfather may have ridden in it at some time or other and they, as well as I, had run a lot of miles in those old cabooses. So I said maybe we should restore it. He was shocked. Really? So we spent the summers of 1999 and 2000 doing it.

The inside was in pretty good shape, about the same as when it was built. It had the original conductor's desk but no drawers, and the stove. The floor under the stove was rotted so we replaced the wood with a quarter inch steel plate that had the same footprint as the sheet metal that it had been sitting on. The stove will still be standing after the caboose is long gone. The outside and windows were another matter. The siding had to be replaced as well as the windows and frames. Two of the rounded corner posts were weathered beyond repair so brother Tom, who knew his way around a carpenter shop, made two new ones. The doors were O.K. It turned out that the windows were basic four-pane barn windows which were pretty close to the right size. You can get them at Menards for your own caboose project.

John's caboose 11546

180

We worked full time both summers. That would be a couple three full days a week. A full day was just under four hours on a good day, with time for a beer and to admire our work at the end of the day. John wanted to paint the caboose bright red. He wanted high gloss fire engine red. I told him that they weren't usually painted that way. Cabooses were various shades of red, depending on what the shops had on hand but never high gloss. Sometimes they were painted barn red. It was John's caboose so it was painted glossy red. John had stencils made for the lettering and the logos, plus the numbers on the sides and over the doors. He usually did things right and it looks pretty official.

Finally we needed a road bed, ties, rails, trucks, and spikes. John got a local landscaper to grade the road bed. I found trucks, one hundred pound rail, ties, fish plates and spikes and we had the stuff trucked in. After the landscapers finished the roadbed they laid the ties and rails and nailed the rails down. We put down forty-four feet of rail. John had a crane come out and they picked up the almost finished caboose and set it on the trucks. Family members assisted with the move. Using measurements from the drovers caboose at the MidContinent Museum I made a CAD drawing of the steps which had been removed when the caboose was delivered and friends helped build and install them. Now I can move the caboose about eight feet back and fourth with a little help from my Farmall H but it isn't quite the same as the old days.

There is a privately owned caboose of the same vintage as John's caboose at North Freedom. It has a cupola and the original passenger train trucks. John got a drawing of his vintage caboose from the North Western Historical Society and from that drawing and measurements from the caboose at North Freedom I made a CAD drawing that could be used for adding a cupola to his caboose. But by that time the only way that would have been done was by telephone and check book. We needed a break.

John Bass

182

Many cabooses were bought over the years by people who had various uses for them. Park them by a stream or in the woods and they made a good get-away or hunter's shack. They were well insulated and handled the weather pretty well. After the Union Pacific bought the North Western, cabooses were no longer sold, probably because of any liability the UP may have felt they might be responsible for or they just didn't want to be bothered.

Old utility caboose at Jefferson Junction painted Zito yellow

John and I looked into the possibility of buying a steel North Western caboose. We found one in Adams but it was in pretty bad shape. There was another one in the Janesville yard but the guys down there said they were still using it. There was and still is a steel caboose at Jefferson Junction but that is used occasionally in winter for the conductor to ride on runs back to the Junction from Fort Atkinson when the caboose is on the point. That is one sad looking caboose. I guess the question was, did we need another caboose?

The village of Butler has a long history of being a railroad town. So when the North Western was sold they gave the village a steel caboose for display purposes. The village never did find a good place for it and it stands in the corner of a park on a very nice road bed and rails, fenced in. It takes a bit of an effort to find it.

After I left the railroad and was working in Chicago I would occasionally commute to Madison on the 400 rather than drive. One Friday afternoon I went aboard and identified myself as a former brakeman out of Madison. The conductor gave me a complimentary ride, which was kind of him since that crew was Wisconsin Division out of Chicago and not Madison Division. I was sitting with the crew chatting when we heard the dreaded **whoosh** of the brakes going into emergency followed almost immediately by the strong smell of gasoline. We knew that every railroad man's nightmare had happened. The crew got on the ground, and I looked up the right side of the train from the trap and saw the front end of a truck. I went over to the other side and saw the back end of a truck. It was one of those big step van delivery trucks, perfectly wrapped around the front of the engine. The crew went up to the front of the train and didn't find the driver in the truck. As they walked back looking for the driver along the road bed I dropped off and went with them. We found the truck's engine in the brush just a little beyond the crossing. A little farther back we found the driver. He had been ejected upon impact. He was lying on his right side in the brush and looked perfectly fine. From the impact side he didn't look good at all.

There was a house on the west side of the crossing. The woman that lived there said the driver had just delivered some bakery goods to her, drove down her driveway and turned left onto the road and right into the path of the train. There were trees and heavy brush along the rail bed and the road so he couldn't have seen the train. It was an unprotected crossing with only cross bucks and he obviously didn't hear the horn, or at least not in time. They had to call out the section crew to pull the truck off the front of the engine. They attached chains to the truck and backed up the train. Another terrible experience for an engine crew.

When the brakes go into emergency sometimes only the guys on the engines know why, sometimes only the men in the caboose or coach know why, and sometimes nobody knows why. All everyone knows is that something potentially bad has happened. If nobody knows why, you've got a busted air line, your train broke in two, or your train is on the ground. If you're in the caboose you want to take a brace, preparing for the worst.

One day in about 1962 Dad's father, Ben, made a trip with him on 507 and 508. They had come in the night before and the next afternoon after I got off work I met them at the depot for dinner. The conductors' room was upstairs in the depot and had lockers for the conductors and

Conductor Roger Bass, top left,
and Ben Bass, seated, second from left

chairs and tables for doing paperwork, reading or playing cards. The guys who ran the scoots, suburban trains, spent time there between runs.

The conductors' room was strictly for conductors. It was their territory. But I guess because I was a blood relative to two conductors I didn't get tossed out. For some reason I had a camera with me so I took the opportunity to make an image of dad and my grandfather, along with some of the other conductors.

There was a trainmen's room in the basement of the depot. I never went down there but occasionally there was some serious poker played there. Every so often railroad officials would get calls from wives whose husbands apparently came home empty-handed on pay day, and then the stakes went down. At least for a while.

As time went by I watched the evolution of North Western power. By the time I left in 1961 the covered wagons had run their course. They were used on the Chicago suburban lines and some of the passenger F units were used in freight service on weekends when they weren't needed for commuter service. Because they were probably geared for passenger service they had to string a lot of them together to pull a long train. They were, of course, still painted in their Zito yellow.

The engines also got more powerful. GE came out with a powerful Dash 8, replacing the old style cabs with comfort cabs, air-conditioned and cushioned from vibration from the rest of the unit. These were followed by Dash 9's and finally an alternating current variation, AC4400CW. Engine crews went from ancient steam engine cabs to an office environment. EMD also went to comfort cabs and produced more powerful engines as well. General Electric is now the nation's largest builder of railroad engines. Incidentally the air-conditioning of the new cabs was probably more for the benefit of the electronics that these engines now use then it was for the comfort of the crews, at least on the C&NW.

The last engine type the North Western bought was the General Electric AC4400CW. These engines used alternating current rather then direct current, which had previously been

AC4400 CW 8819 with C&NW signature slogan OPERATION LIFESAVER

pretty much universally used. They, like the earlier Dash 9's, had a distinctive lightning strip paint job which some guys liked and others weren't real pleased with. I thought they looked pretty distinctive.

The Chicago and North Western flag lasted from 1848 to 1995 and was the oldest legacy railroad in the nation when it was bought by the UP, and still is. The Union Pacific will match that record in 2009 and will take over that honor in 2010.

While it wasn't unique I was one of the guys that worked the crease between the steam and diesel eras. Because the newly built Interstate Highway System was covering more of the nation it also marked the end of a lot of way freights, that business taken over by trucks. Better highways and newer planes drained the railroad passenger business. The highly successful Boeing 707 jet went into service in 1958. Rail passenger service was reduced to high traffic corridors between eastern cities and in suburban service. Amtrak took over cross country passenger service. Passenger service almost always ran at a loss. Freight service supported it. Now taxpayers cover the cost for Amtrak that freight trains used to do. Some congressmen think that Amtrak should operate at least at break even.

That will probably never happen.

John Bass

End of the line

John's caboose 11546

Employee number

FORM 1647   R-51073 3M 2-52

C. & N. W. RY. CO.

NAME_____Charles A. Bass_____

SOCIAL SECURITY No._____

ACCOUNT No._____8037_____

EMPLOYED ON THE_____Madison-Wis._____DIVISION

EMPLOYES TIME IS RECORDED BY NAME AND ACCOUNT NUMBER
BOTH NAME AND ACCOUNT NUMBER MUST BE
SHOWN ON TIME SLIPS.

Record of physical exams

Form 3854   R-48156 15M 4-51 ARB

IDENTIFICATION
CHICAGO & NORTH WESTERN RAILWAY CO.
Certificate of Re-Examination

Name _Chas. Bass_
Address _Madison_
Occupation _Brakeman_   Div. _Madison_

DATE	EXAMINING SURGEON
APR 18 1955	Geo. A. Benish
6-12-56	Albert Tormey
6-27-57	
6-25-58	Albert Tormey
6-25-59	G.A. Benish

This card must be in possession of employe at all times for inspection if required

Accident report instructions

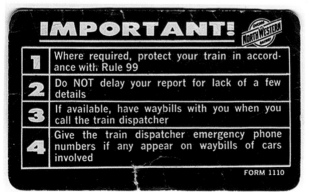

IMPORTANT!

1	Where required, protect your train in accordance with Rule 99
2	Do NOT delay your report for lack of a few details
3	If available, have waybills with you when you call the train dispatcher
4	Give the train dispatcher emergency phone numbers if any appear on waybills of cars involved

FORM 1110

190

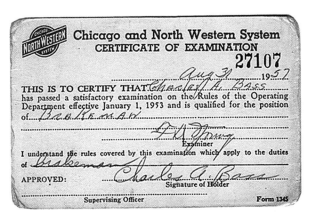

CHICAGO & NORTH WESTERN RY.

Name _Charles A. Bass_ Code Figure _1_

Soc. Sec. Number _____ Working Number _8037_

U.S. Treasury Department Form W-4 (Revised 1954) required by the Internal Revenue Code of 1954 has been filed by the above named employe with the Auditor Disbursements. The figure indicating total exemption claimed should be shown on all payrolls. No further filing of Form W-4 is required until exemption status is changed. R. R. Retirement Board Form CER-1 also has been filed. _Madison_

Filed By _____ Divn. _33-1_ First Half 19

Form No. 1564 Roll No. Effective Date

Record of W-4 form for railroad retirement

Chicago and North Western System
CERTIFICATE OF EXAMINATION

27107

Aug 31 19_57_

THIS IS TO CERTIFY THAT _Charles A. Bass_ has passed a satisfactory examination on the Rules of the Operating Department effective January 1, 1953 and is qualified for the position of _BRAKEMAN_

Examiner

I understand the rules covered by this examination which apply to the duties of _Brakeman_

APPROVED: _Charles A. Bass_
Signature of Holder

Supervising Officer Form 1345

Book of rules sign-off

TRAIN ACCIDENT REPORTING INSTRUCTIONS

In case of collision or derailment, Conductor (or other crew member) will report the following to the train dispatcher in accordance with Form 1108-B:

1. Date and time of accident
2. Location (distance from nearest station)
3. Nature of accident
4. Weather conditions
5. Train(s) involved: (No., Condr., Engr., Loads, Empties, Speed)
6. No. of units/cars derailed
7. Location of derailed cars in train
8. Are derailed units/cars upright, leaning or tipped?
9. Is main track blocked
10. Is other track available to get around derailment?
11. Personal injuries, if any
12. Assumed cause of accident
13. Other information
14. Initials and numbers of cars and contents

Accident report instructions

Copies of this book may be purchased from the author, and remarks addressed to him, at

CBassf20@aol.com

or

Charles A. Bass
117 Red Fox Drive
Johnson Creek, WI 53038